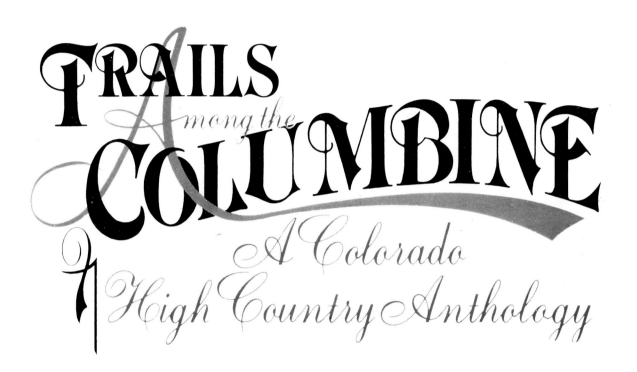

# TRAILS Among the COLUMBINE

## A Colorado High Country Anthology

# 1990

SUNDANCE
Books

# ~ *PREFACE* ~

COLORADO'S STORY is replete with the impossible becoming possible.... The quest for gold and silver sparkles like glittering threads through the tales and traditions of Colorado's early pioneer days.

The lure of gold and silver is woven into a gigantic patchwork quilt portrayed against a background of towering snow-crowned mountain peaks. And through these rugged-and-rocky peaks legendary narrow-gauge railroads wound their way — reaching even the most remote regions of the Columbine State.

Hundreds of books have been published about Colorado's romantic past — about the many exciting aspects of "the impossible dream," the wild "boom" periods it initiated, and the frenetic excitment it ignited. However, none of these books combine the written word with lavish pictorial documentation in quite the dramatic way that the *Trails Among the Columbine* series does.

What this continuing series presents is lavish in both depth and scope. Unlike typical books about Colorado and its dramatic past, Sundance Publications and the writers who produced it have carefully chosen photographs, maps and other illustrations to weave the total content into a precise and detailed story — like a beautifully embellished tapestry — a tapestry with a richness of feeling, providing one with a truly sumptuous visual experience.

Colorado is unique among the mountain regions of the American West. Other Western states have single mountain ranges, which when surpassed, are left behind. However, the Colorado Rockies consist of many complicated ranges, extending from east to west for over 300 miles. After passing through the eastern foothills — which abruptly rise up from the Great Plains — one dramatically ascends the Front Range to cross the great Continental Divide. From the top of the Divide one can behold mountain range upon mountain range to the west — as far as the eye can see. This immense complexity of mountain ranges includes 52 peaks with an elevation of 14,000 feet or more, as well as hundreds which rise to over 12,000 feet. This region of rugged grandeur is bisected or interposed by countless valleys, deep cañons and picturesque parklands.

With today's modern highways, it is relatively easy to traverse this jumbled-and-abstruse region, and it is truly difficult to imagine how the early prospectors found their way through this complex-and-inhibiting country. And even after they discovered promising "color" in the streams and among the rocky crags, it is even more incomprehensible how they managed to process and transport their ore to the outside world — to say nothing of how they replenished their food, clothing and other supplies.

Although my grandparents were Colorado pioneers, and I traveled over many of the rough mountain roads before they were paved, it is hard for me to imagine how the early gold seekers endured the hardships they obviously had to withstand. Their audacious ventures virtually defy comprehension. This is made painfully obvious any time one bounces over an old wagon road in a four-wheel-drive vehicle — going up awesome grades, impossible for ordinary automobiles to traverse. Whenever one looks up to see shafthouses clinging to the sheer sides of rocky cliffs, one can only wonder what compelled these men to undertake such hazardous enterprises.

Obviously, the dream of finding gold and silver in Colorado's high country superseded fears of failure — to say nothing of the very real risks to life and limb.

As early placer mining gave way to lode mining, shafts and drifts (tunnels) were driven into the mountains throughout Colorado's mineral belt. And as refractory ores became commonplace, large reduction mills and smelters had to be erected to process the complex ores. And it was not long before narrow-gauge railroads became a necessary ingredient in Colorado's mining economy. During the 1880's and '90's little mountain-climbing railroads penetrated nearly every part of western Colorado. The narrow-gauge roads twisted their way between the high peaks and up the rocky gulches in order to reach virtually every mining camp of any importance in the state.

This volume continues to relate the story of Colorado's high-country towns and the diminutive three-foot-gauge railroads that tied them together and allowed them to reach the outside world.*

Russ Collman, Author

---

* *Note:* To acquaint the reader with the Gunnison Country and the area just to the north of it, a few previously published books from Sundance Publications should be mentioned. Gunnison and partial coverage of the Crested Butte area — including the Ohio Pass and Kebler Pass areas — are found in the 1989 edition of *Trails Among the Columbine*. On the north side of the Elk Mountain Range, Crystal City, Marble, Aspen, Ashcroft and the Roaring Fork drainages have been covered extensively in *The Crystal River Pictorial*, *Aspen On the Roaring Fork* (out of print) and *The Roaring Fork Valley*. The object of Ron Ruhoff's story in this edition is to fill in missing gaps between these areas.

**SUNDANCE** PUBLICATIONS *Ltd*

250 Broadway • Denver, Colorado 80203

**Published by**
Sundance Publications, Ltd., Denver, Colorado

**Graphical Presentation and Printing by**
Sundance Publications, Ltd., Denver, Colorado

**Typesetting by**
LaserWriting, Inc., Denver, Colorado

*Production Manager – Dell A. McCoy*

*Photographic Director – Steven J. Meyers*

*Editorial Consultant – Ed Haley*

ISBN  0-913582-51-4

*SPECIAL ACKNOWLEGMENT – –*

The publisher gratefully acknowledges the gener-
ous gift of time and expertise given to this book
project by Ed Haley.

E. J. HALEY PHOTO

**FRONT COVER** — Denver & Rio Grande Western Engine 483 was taking on water at the Sargent tank on May 2, 1955, in preparation for the return to Salida. This was the last D&RGW freight train operated over Marshall Pass. Notice the Fairmont section car, which had been set off the rails of the mainline.

BETTY LeMASSENA PHOTO

**BACK COVER** — Robert A. LeMassena was handing up a can containing water to "Doc" Turner to cool the radiator of their D&RGW section car. They had the privilege of making nearly the last trip by rail over Marshall Pass prior to abandonment of the line.

# TABLE OF CONTENTS

RON RUHOFF PHOTO

**COLORADO'S BLUE COLUMBINE** — shown here in the high country of the Centennial State — was adopted by the General Assembly in 1899 as the official State flower. July usually is the best time of the year to view the beautiful blue columbine at elevations above 7,000 feet.

# D&RG STATION MAP
# SALIDA, COLORADO
## Milepost 216 At Depot
### — 1889 —

*Salida.*

ALIGNMENT OF THE D. & R. G. R. R. OVER MARSHALL PASS.

RIO GRANDE
ROYAL GORGE
MOFFAT TUNNEL
SCENIC LINE OF THE WORLD

1936 – 1945

# VIA MARSHALL PASS TO GUNNISON
## — Over the Denver & Rio Grande Railway —
### "The Scenic Line of the World"
### By Russ Collman

**T**HE YEAR 1881 was the Denver & Rio Grande's greatest period of glory. In no other year did the D&RG lay as much rail. Not only was the transmountain line to the great Salt Lake begun, but General William Jackson Palmer's narrow-gauge railroad took up residence at the new Denver Union Depot, and conversion to standard gauge was started on the mainline along the Front Range of the Rockies.

The young Civil War brigadier general — who won his star while still in his 20's — began dreaming about building his very own railroad not long after he returned from managing the Kansas Pacific Railroad's survey to the West Coast in 1867. The cavalry general had laid out a route between the Great Plains and San Francisco Bay by way of the Rocky Mountains and the Sierra Nevadas, and he had become familiar with the vastness of the American West. In 1868, General Palmer was appointed in charge of construction for the Kansas Pacific line from Lawrence, Kansas, to the infant city of Denver — at the foot of Colorado's spectacular mountain escarpment. And the booming mining camps of Colorado Territory were eagerly awaiting the arrival of the first railroad from the east.

The standard-gauge Kansas Pacific reached Denver on August 15, 1870. Shortly thereafter, on November 7, 1870, General Palmer married Mary "Queen" Mellen — and immediately after the wedding, the couple left for a honeymoon tour of the British Isles. While the general was in Britain, he visited the narrow-gauge railways of Wales, his first exposure to rail lines where the gauge was less than the standard 4 feet, 8½ inches apart.

Upon the general's return to Denver, he quickly plunged into building what he called the Denver & Rio Grande Railway. It was shortly prior to the general's marriage and trip to Britain — on October 27, 1870 — that this infant enterprise was officially incorporated in Colorado Territory. The preliminary survey for what was to become the D&RG had been accomplished during February of 1870, in connection with constructing the Kansas Pacific. This was for a route between Denver and Colorado Springs;

however, the KP was never built beyond Denver. Instead, General Palmer began grading on this line during the spring of 1871, and the first track was spiked down at Milepost 0 in Denver on July 1, 1871. And the first three-foot narrow-gauge trackage of the D&RG was completed to the new town of Colorado Springs on October 20, 1871.

Subsequently, D&RG trackage was completed into Trinidad (near the southern Colorado border); into the San Luis Valley to Alamosa, Antonito, and Española, New Mexico (a relatively short distance away from Santa Fé), which later became a branch line off of the San Juan Extension to Durango and Silverton. From Pueblo, the D&RG set out to reach the booming Leadville silver-mining district, which it accomplished during July of 1880 — at Malta (Milepost 271.0, Elevation 9,580 feet), about four miles west of Leadville. At about the same time, the beginning of what later became the Gunnison Extension was started, as five miles of trackage was laid between Salida and Poncha Junction.

## BUILDING THE MARSHALL PASS LINE

**SALIDA** ("exit" or "outlet" in Spanish) — Milepost 215.1, Elevation 7,050 feet — was the junction point on the Denver & Rio Grande for the Gunnison Extension. Situated just outside the western end of the Arkansas Cañon, Salida was also the principal terminus of both the Monarch Branch and the line over Poncha Pass to the iron mine at Orient, located in the San Luis Valley. And, of course, Salida was the starting point for the line over Tennessee Pass and beyond — the first transmountain route standard-gauged by the D&RG.

As new income from Leadville traffic enriched the Denver & Rio Grande, General Palmer perceived a threat from the expanding Denver, South Park & Pacific Railroad, another Colorado narrow-gauge railroad. The DSP&P had been established in 1872 as a route to connect Denver with the mining districts to the west of the "Mile High City." Of course, the South Park line had an aspiration to go beyond the western border of Colorado... and ultimately reach the West Coast, as the railroad's corporate name suggested.

JOHN W. MAXWELL PHOTO

**THIS EXCURSION TRAIN** of the Rocky Mountain Railroad Club was about to leave Salida on September 18, 1948, headed for Marshall Pass and Gunnison. The Denver & Rio Grande Western's "Silver Vista" observation car had been coupled on the rear end of the train for the best viewing enjoyment of passengers — as the train rounded curves on the historic narrow-gauge route the excursion was about to traverse.

In October of 1879, Governor John Evans, president of the DSP&P, and General Palmer, president of the D&RG, had negotiated an agreement regarding their proposed routes to Leadville and Gunnison. The agreement allowed the DSP&P to operate via D&RG trackage between Buena Vista and Leadville, while the D&RG was permitted access into the Gunnison Country by way of DSP&P rails.

Unfortunately, the Union Pacific's manipulative chief executive, Jay Gould, bought the South Park line during November of 1880. As long as Governor Evans had controlled the DSP&P, General Palmer believed his D&RG could cooperate with this similar Colorado narrow-gauge railroad. However, when Jay Gould and the massive Union Pacific entered the picture, the entire scene changed. In short order, the joint operating agreement between the D&RG and the DSP&P was cancelled by General Palmer. This left the DSP&P without an easy entrance into Leadville's silver-rich bonanza area, and it immediately ignited a heated race to reach the potential wealth of the Gunnison Country.

Typical of all the mining districts of Colorado, the Gunnison region was largely isolated from the population centers just east of the Front Range prior to the arrival of the railroad. However, the D&RG and the DSP&P needed more than hyperbolic claims about the precious-mineral riches of the Gunnison Country. While it was true that gold-and-silver mines had made Gunnison the main supply town and shipping center of the region, high-quality bituminous and anthracite coal deposits to the north of Gunnison appeared to be of greater interest to the railroads than precious minerals. Not only did the railroads require increasing amounts of coal for their steam engines, but the new and growing smelters, steel mills and other industries of the Front Range cities were beginning to devour many tons of coal.

Beyond Gunnison, the booming San Juan region of southwestern Colorado beckoned. And to the west of Colorado was the transcontinental route to Salt Lake City and the highly alluring, burgeoning population centers of California.

Before the autumn of 1880 came to Colorado's high country, the D&RG had decided on the route

OTTO C. PERRY PHOTO – E. J. HALEY COLLECTION

THE REGULARLY SCHEDULED passenger train between Salida and Montrose was named the "Shavano." Here, the train was making its last westbound run on a cold winter morning, November 24, 1940. The train was being hauled by Denver & Rio Grande Western K-28 2–8–2 No. 479. Passengers were allowed time to eat at the hotel lunchroom in Salida before boarding the train for their journey over Marshall Pass and down the grade to Gunnison. (Notice the LUNCH ROOM sign on the corner of the hotel.) The "Shavano" was steaming slowly past the Salida depot (out of view to the left) and the Hotel Monte Cristo (right), as it rolled over the sharp curve leading to the through-truss bridge over the Arkansas River.

ON SEPTEMBER 25, 1949, the Rocky Mountain Railroad Club chartered an excursion train out of Salida, bound for the end of the Monarch Branch — then back to Mears Junction and south over Poncha Pass to Villa Grove, and return to Salida. D&RGW locomotive No. 499, a K-37 2–8–2, was pulling out of the Salida station and crossing the bridge over the Arkansas River, a short distance out of the Arkansas Cañon. Tenderfoot Hill is in the background.

JACK A. PFEIFER PHOTO – E. J. HALEY COLLECTION

5220 HOTEL MONTE CHRISTO SALIDA COLO. W.H.J. & Co.

for its first crossing of the continent's Great Divide. The new route definitely would be constructed over 10,880-foot Marshall Pass. Otto Mears' decision to sell his toll road over Marshall Pass was the determing factor. The D&RG agreed to pay Mears $13,000 for his rather rough wagon road over the Divide. More importantly, the Mears toll road provided the D&RG with access to the Gunnison Country, as well as control of the route, while the railroad was under construction.

By the end of September, 1880, the D&RG had made its first move in building the Gunnison Extension when a railroad pile-driver finished hammering timbers into the bed of the Arkansas River at Salida. This bridge was completed shortly thereafter, and by November 22, 1880, passenger service began to Poncha Junction.

*(Continued on Page 16)*

## DENVER & RIO GRANDE RAILROAD
## TIME TABLE – 1898

# Denver & Rio Grande Railroad.

### TRAINS BETWEEN GRAND JUNCTION AND DENVER.

| STATIONS. | Miles from Gunnison. | EAST. | | | | Read Up. |
|---|---|---|---|---|---|---|
| | | No. 8 Atlantic Express D | No. 10 East'rn Ex. D | No. 24 Way Freig't S E. | No. 22 Thro' Freig't D | |
| Denver | 290.3 | 8 45 | 7 10 | * | 2 45 | |
| Pueblo | 170.7 | 3 55 | 2 20 | * | 3 15 | |
| Salida........N | 73.8 | ‡ 11 55 | lv 10 20 | 5 00 | lv 5 50 | |
| | | 11 30 | ar 10 08 | | ar 4 05 | |
| Poncha Junction......D | 68.8 | * 11 17 | * 9 55 | 4 38 | 3 40 | |
| Otto.. | 64.3 | 10 59 | 9 36 | 4 09 | 3 13 | |
| Mears Junction......D | 62.8 | * 10 53 | * 9 30 | 4 00 | 3 05 | |
| Shirley | 60.6 | † 10 45 | 9 20 | 3 42 | 2 43 | |
| Keene | 56.9 | 10 28 | 9 05 | 3 20 | 2 17 | |
| Gray's.. .........D | 54 8 | † 10 20 | 8 58 | 3 08 | 2 05 | |
| Pocono | 51.3 | 10 05 | 8 43 | 2 45 | 1 40 | |
| Marshall Pass........N | 48.1 | lv 9 50 | lv 8 30 | lv 2‡25 | lv 1 20 | |
| | | ar 9 43 | ar 8 22 | ar 2 10 | ar 1 05 | |
| Hillden | 45.0 | 9 27 | 8 07 | 1 45 | 12 43 | |
| Shawano........D | 43.9 | 9 18 | 8 02 | 1 35 | 12 35 | |
| Chester........D | 40.2 | 9 02 | 7 45 | 1 12 | 12 08 | |
| Buxton | 36.0 | 8 43 | 7 27 | 12 45 | 11 45 | |
| Sargent........N | 31.4 | lv 8 30 | lv 7 15 | lv 12 20 | lv 11 00 | |
| | | ar 8 25 | ar 7 10 | ar 11 59 | ar 11 20 | |
| Elko | 26.8 | 8 14 | 7 00 | 11 36 | 10 38 | |
| Crookton | 23.1 | 8 07 | 6 52 | 11 17 | 10 22 | |
| Doyle | 19.2 | † 7 57 | 6 43 | 10 56 | 10 04 | |
| Bonita | 18.2 | 7 54 | 6 40 | 10 51 | 9 59 | |
| Parlin........D | 11.8 | † 7 40 | 6 27 | 10 04 | 9 22 | |
| Mounds | 6 5 | 7 28 | 6 15 | 9 35 | 8 58 | |
| Gunnison........N | 134.9 | 7 15 | + 6 00 | lv 9 00 | lv 8 30 | |

**THE HOTEL MONTE CRISTO** in Salida occupied this frame structure beside the Denver & Rio Grande mainline, which came out of the Arkansas Cañon at Salida — en route from Denver to Salt Lake City, in this scene photographed during 1883. The hotel offered overnight lodging and dining service for those who wished to catch trains for towns such as Leadville, Monarch, Gunnison and points to either the east or west. The D&RG's passenger depot was built of stone — and this attractive building occupied space west of the line to Leadville at this division point on the railroad. In the lower view, a horse-drawn coach (called an omnibus) and wagons were waiting for fares bound for the town of Salida, as passengers disembarked from a standard-gauge passenger train at the Hotel Monte Cristo.

NO. 202. SALIDA FROM THE EAST, D.&R.G.R.R. MELLEN PHOTO.

**OPPOSITE (above):** In 1890, Salida was an important division point on the Denver & Rio Grande Railway. Downtown Salida is located across the Arkansas River from the railroad. The wooden Howe truss-type bridge (to the right) carried the track headed toward both Marshall Pass and Monarch. Salida's *second* narrow-gauge roundhouse and shop (in the foreground) kept motive power in operation. There were 27 stalls in this new roundhouse, according to the D&RG station map of 1889 (printed on Page 6).

**OPPOSITE (below):** Denver & Rio Grande trackage had just recently reached Salida when this view of about 1881 was photographed. It portrays the railroad's first roundhouse (with 14 stalls), as well as the coaling trestle. By 1889, a new — and much larger — brick-and-stone roundhouse had replaced the original roundhouse.

**THE D&RG MAINLINE** to Leadville and points west, was converted to dual gauge in 1890. The Marshall Pass line crossed the Arkansas River and provided access to industries and warehouses in the town of Salida. Three-rail track had been installed in Salida to permit the use of standard-gauge cars at these freight sidings.

**THIS VIEW OF SALIDA** was taken about 1895, as the photographer looked south over the town from Tenderfoot Hill. The Arkansas River runs through the middle of the picture. To the far left, the large three-story D&RG hospital can be seen above the water tank. A string of narrow-gauge coal cars stood just beyond the tank. The Rio Grande superintendent's house is on this side of the tracks, across from the Hotel Monte Cristo.

THE FOUR-STORY ST. CLAIR HOTEL can be seen on this page (center left). A small section of "F" Street in downtown Salida is visible at the bridge crossing over the Arkansas River, behind the depot. Two boxcars and two loaded gondolas were standing on the D&RG bridge, which carried mainline trackage across the river. These cars had been part of a freight train, which had recently arrived in town. The D&RG's Salida switcher would sort them out later.

15

**PONCHA JUNCTION** — Milepost 220.1, Elevation 7,481 feet — had a depot and a passing siding with 52-car capacity. At this point, connections were made with Sanderson stagecoaches, which used the Mears toll road over Marshall Pass for entry into the sprawling Gunnison Country. The railroad's 4.0-percent ruling grade to the summit began here.

On November 18, 1880, the temperature fell to a chilling 23 degrees below zero at Salida, and it was even colder up along the line being graded toward Marshall Pass. Thereupon, workers assigned to grading and tracklaying gangs quit in droves, and although some work continued throughout the winter, tracklaying slowed to a crawl.

*(Continued on Page 26)*

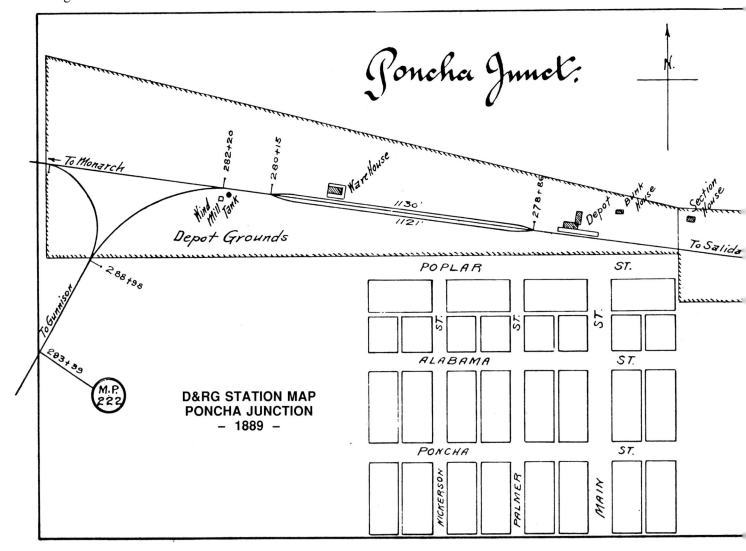

D&RG STATION MAP
PONCHA JUNCTION
– 1889 –

JOSEPH SCHICK PHOTO – E. J. HALEY COLLECTION

**THE PONCHA JUNCTION DEPOT** was constructed on the north side of the D&RG mainline, between Salida and Mears Junction, at Milepost 220.1. The photographer aimed his camara toward Salida, showing the distant section house in the view (at left). Above, the bunkhouse sat behind the depot. Below, on April 8, 1950, engine No. 489, a Class K-36 2–8–2, was approaching the depot during a heavy snowfall. Notice that the semaphore blades of the train-order signal have been removed.

**OVERLEAF:** Mount Shavano rises above the Arkansas Valley near the left side of the right-hand page. William H. Jackson's photographic special occupied the mainline, which had been heading downgrade toward Poncha Junction, after the Jackson party had toured the Marshall Pass line. Jackson had been taking publicity photographs for the Denver & Rio Grande Railway. Notice that Jackson gave the Spanish masculine gender ending for Poncha Pass, spelling the name "Poncho" (which means "cape").

W. H. JACKSON PHOTO – RICHARD A. RONZIO COLLECTION

ROBERT W. RICHARDSON – COLORADO RAILROAD MUSEUM COLLECTION

3497. MT SHAVANO FROM PONCHO PASS. W.H.JC.

ROBERT W. RICHARDSON caught this three-engine freight train, with one boxcar and a long string of empty gondolas, as it struggled up the 4.0-percent grade between Poncha Junction and Mears Junction. He was fortunate enough to be on hand on March 22, 1950, to record this dramatic view. The train was en route to Gunnison via Marshall Pass.

ABOVE, D&RGW NO. 498 was drifting downgrade from Poncha Pass on April 21, 1940, with an assortment of gondolas, two Texaco double-dome tankcars and boxcars.

OPPOSITE (above): Not far below Otto, Train 315 — the "Shavano" — was photographed with D&RGW Engine 479 on the head end, as it blasted its way up the steep grade to Marshall Pass on May 5, 1940. Below (left), locomotive No. 492 was hauling stock cars, the "Silver Vista" car and coaches over Poncha Pass on November 4, 1949. The passenger cars were being returned to Alamosa after being used on the Rocky Mountain Railroad Club's Salida–Monarch–Villa Grove excursion trip of September 25, 1949.

EN ROUTE TO SALIDA, D&RGW locomotive No. 489 was hauling a long string of gondolas loaded with scrap rail from the Gunnison region. The train was photographed as it drifted over Poncha Pass. The 2–8–2 was crossing Poncha Creek on the steel girder bridge above Otto. The date was May 24, 1955.

OPPOSITE (above): The station of Otto was situated at Milepost 223.9, 8.8 miles west of Salida and 64.5 miles east of Gunnison. In this view you are looking down the weedy main track, with the passing track on the right. There was never anything more than a passing siding at Otto. This station was listed at Milepost 226 on the D&RG's 1889 station map (at right on this page). Below (opposite), the same string of empties that appeared on Pages 20–21 was heading westbound out of Salida, going upgrade, and was passing through Otto during 1950.

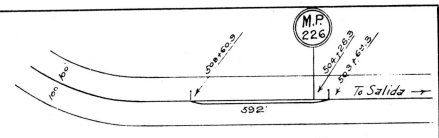

**D&RG STATION MAP – OTTO – 1889**

ROBERT W. RICHARDSON PHOTO – COLORADO RAILROAD MUSEUM

**ON JANUARY 28, 1949,** a flanger train was dispatched out of Salida to clear snow off the track over Poncha Pass. Near Otto, Numbers 499 and 496 were seen with Caboose 0586 and a "drag" flanger as they crossed the 54-foot bridge above Otto.

## MEARS JUNCTION TO ORIENT

**AT THE SAME TIME** tracklayers were busy spiking down steel over Marshall Pass, other track workers were busy laying rail south of Mears Junction over 9,059-foot Poncha Pass to Villa Grove and the iron-ore mine at Orient. Before the winter of 1881 closed in on the San Luis Valley, the 28-mile Iron Mine Branch had been completed, and an "accommodation" passenger train had been put into service. The Iron Mine Branch was later called the San Luis Branch — and even later, came to be commonly referred to as the "Valley Line."

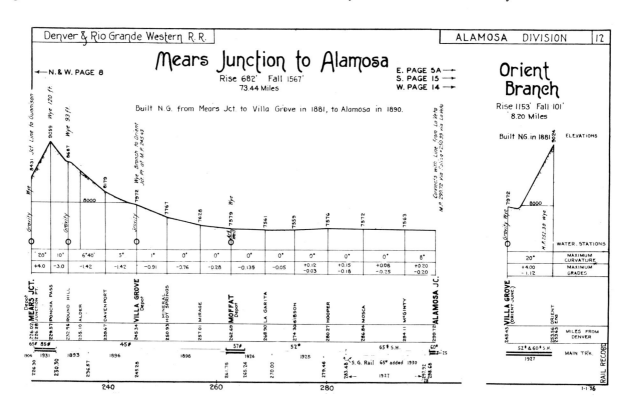

**MEARS JUNCTION** was located 11 miles southwest of Salida. In 1882, the photographer aimed his camera up Poncha Creek, toward the snow-covered peaks surrounding Marshall Pass — capturing this view on his glass-plate negative. A small frame depot sat across the track from a welcome hotel; however, the nearby grounds were cluttered with scrap wood strewn around by workers at the adjacent sawmill.

**MEARS JUNCTION** — Milepost 226.0, Elevation 8,431 feet — was 62.4 miles east of Gunnison. At this point, the Iron Mine Branch left the original east-west mainline and ascended through heavily forested hills to Poncha Pass.

*(Continued on Page 36)*

27

ON NOVEMBER 4, 1949, five cars of coal were being pushed upgrade toward Poncha Pass — in this view photographed above Mears Junction. And to the right, the 482 was pulling a train upgrade at Mears Junction on February 14, 1951, bound for Alamosa.

OPPOSITE: The old water tank at Mears Junction held water for several years after rail was removed from the line.

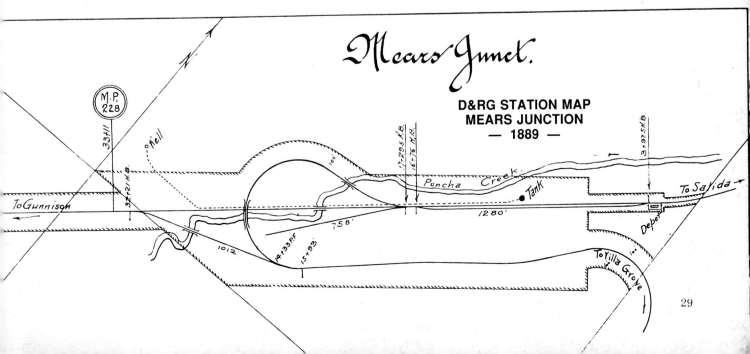

*Mears Junct.*

D&RG STATION MAP
MEARS JUNCTION
— 1889 —

M.P.
228

To Gunnison

Poncha Creek

Tank

To Salida

Depot

To Villa Grove

THE THREE VIEWS included here illustrate Mears Junction. Above, a construction train was returning to Salida over the newly completed trestle at the junction in 1881. The shiny new Class 60 2–8–0 was No. 83, a Baldwin product of 1881. Poncha Creek is in view at lower left on Page 30. The Marshall Pass mainline ran beneath the Iron Mine (Villa Grove) Branch at this location, as it headed toward Gunnison. Lower photograph (left): No. 480 had 16 cars in tow when photographed at Mears Junction, headed for Alamosa on November 25, 1950. Below, a string of five loaded gondolas were in a train that was doubling the hill during 1950, with No. 492 providing motive power on that afternoon so many years ago. Trains headed north from the San Luis Valley could turn west to head toward Gunnison by using the steep track that went under the wooden trestle — plainly in view in all of these scenes.

ROBERT W. RICHARDSON PHOTO – COLORADO RAILROAD MUSEUM

ON THE OPPOSING PAGE, the same train seen on Pages 20 and 24 was photographed during 1950, as it headed for Alamosa. It had just reached Mears Junction and had encircled the loop over the mainline to Marshall Pass. Loaded coal cars occupy the spur in the middle of the loop. Above, a Rocky Mountain Railroad Club excursion train — headed by No. 499 — had been chartered on September 25, 1949, and was southbound, heading for Villa Grove at Mears Junction. Below, on February 14, 1951, Engine 480 was making a "caboose hop" to Alamosa, and she was photographed as she crossed over the trestle at Mears Junction.

**AT PONCHA PASS**, Train 61, southbound, had pulled to a stop so that the helper locomotive, No. 408, could be uncoupled and turned on the wye for the return trip to Salida. The D&RG used link-and-pin couplers until 1903, as shown here shortly after 1890. Notice the curtain lettered "174," which covered the oil headlight on the passenger train's engine. This black curtain was used on oil-burning headlights when the waiting engine was on a siding, meeting an oncoming train. The headlight was adorned with steer horns and the front of the 4–6–0 was graced with a large white star. During this period, engineers were assigned to specific locomotives, and furnished their own headlamps. After lining up the switch, the fireman of No. 408 would have a less strenuous job going back downgrade. Mount Ouray is above the passenger train.

**LOCOMOTIVE NO. 489** was photographed as she headed north on the so-called "Valley Line," while turning a Rocky Mountain Railroad Club excursion train on the Villa Grove wye. The majestic western slopes of the Sangre de Cristo Mountains can be seen in the background. She had been hauling an excursion train from Salida in 1950. This branch had been constructed to Orient (originally called Iron Mine) in 1881, and left the mainline at this wye. North of Alamosa, the broad San Luis Valley — an ancient lake bed — contained a 53-mile stretch of straight track, completely without curves; however, this part of the line was not completed until 1890.

**PONCHA PASS** — Milepost 229.6, Elevation 9,059 feet — was the first station south of Mears Junction. This pass was the primary northern entrance to the broad San Luis Valley. There was a 33-car passing siding here, as well as a wye for turning helpers, but little else. Ute Indians were the first to regularly use this relatively low pass, and Otto Mears had constructed a toll road across the pass in 1867.

OTTO C. PERRY PHOTO – RICHARD A. RONZIO COLLECTION

**NORTH OF VILLA GROVE, a Salida-bound freight train was climbing the grade to Poncha Pass on October 7, 1945, with extra flags flying on Engine 497. The distant Sangre de Cristo Mountains appear on the horizon at left.**

**ROUND HILL** — Milepost 232.9, Elevation 8,687 feet — had a water tank and was a siding often used for work cars. The siding could hold 46 cars. South of Round Hill, the D&RG roughly paralled the Sangre de Cristo Range (to the east of the railroad).

**VILLA GROVE** — Milepost 245.3, Elevation 7,972 feet — was originally a ranch center, with a population of about 125, typical of the small settlements in the more remote areas of Colorado — with only one main street and a few small business buildings. The D&RG had a small water tank here, as well as a passing siding and wye. The siding had a capacity of 45 cars. (The small water tank at Villa Grove came from Jacks Cabin, which was moved from there when the D&RG's Gunnison lines were abandoned.)

The original branch, built in 1881, turned east at Villa Grove and continued to the east slope of the Sangre de Cristo Mountains, which rise abruptly from the valley floor. The trackage terminated at an iron-ore mine, about 8.2 miles from Villa Grove.

**ORIENT** (originally called Iron Mine) — Milepost 253.5, Elevation 9,024 feet — was the terminus of the branch, and was the location of the only major iron-ore mine in Colorado. The Colorado Coal & Iron Company (the predecessor of the Colorado Fuel & Iron Corporation) developed this mine as a source of iron ore for its steel mill at Pueblo. The mine produced continuously for CF&I for over 50 years, employing over 100 miners. By the time the D&RG reached here in 1881, there were two cafés,

at least one saloon and several other commercial enterprises. By 1900, the population was about 400. An average of 200 tons of ore was shipped out of here daily over the narrow-gauge line to Pueblo.

The miners who lived here had quite a breathtaking view of the broad San Luis Valley from their homes in Orient. However, nothing is left here today but the abandoned mine dumps.

In 1890 the D&RG extended the Iron Mine Branch some 54 miles from Villa Grove to Alamosa. This was accomplished mainly to provide a connection between the northern and southern narrow-gauge sections of the railroad — after the third rail was removed between Walsenburg and Pueblo, following an earlier removal of the third rail between Salida and Pueblo. After this extension was completed through the relatively flat San Luis Valley, the route became known as the "Valley Line." Having no curves for 53 miles, this extension had the fifth-longest tangent in the United States.

*(Continued on Page 40)*

**—— D&RG 1882 TIME TABLE ——**
**Denver – Villa Grove – Hot Springs**
**SAN LUIS BRANCH**

| SOUTHWARD. | | STATIONS. | Miles. | NORTHWARD. | |
|---|---|---|---|---|---|
| | Express. | | | Express. | |
| .......... | 7 30 p.m. | Lv.....Denver.....Ar. | ... | 7 05 a.m. | .......... |
| .......... | 1 25 a.m. | " .South Pueblo.. ' | 120 | 12 40 " | .......... |
| .......... | 8 00 " | " .....Salida..... " | 217 | 6 48 p.m. | .......... |
| .......... | 9 18 " | " .....Mears..... " | 228 | 5 30 " | .......... |
| .......... | 9 48 " | " ..Poncho Pass..Lv. | 231 | 5 00 " | .......... |
| .......... | 10 18 " | " ...Round Hill.. " | 234 | 4 30 " | .......... |
| .......... | 11 59 " | " ...Villa Grove... " | 247 | 3 20 " | .......... |
| .......... | 12 55 p.m | Ar...Hot Springs..Lv. | 255 | 2 25 " | .......... |

THE TOWN OF VILLA GROVE was on the D&RG's "Valley Line," at the "Golden Gate" of the San Luis Valley. Situated near the foot of Poncha Pass, Villa Grove is at an elevation of 7,972 feet. The 8.2-mile spur to Orient (and the iron-ore mine) connected here, and an estimated 100 to 200 tons of iron ore were shipped daily from the CF&I's mining operation. Incidentally, the connecting wye was called "Orient Junction," although it was part of the station of Villa Grove. (See the D&RG profile on Page 26.)

EAST OF VILLA GROVE — at Orient — the Colorado Fuel & Iron Corporation developed a company town. The resulting views shown on these two pages were shot near the end-of-track. The company-owned store at Orient furnished groceries, clothing, hardware and household items for the townsfolk of this isolated settlement.

THE 1920'S VIEW of Orient shown below illustrates the living conditions miners' families endured before indoor plumbing made life easier. Immigrant labor occupied most of these camps operated by CF&I. People found the job and town — primitive as it was — an improvement over what they had left in Europe.

**THE LAST WESTBOUND FREIGHT TRAIN over Marshall Pass consisted of a long string of about 55 empty gondolas, dispatched from Salida to Sargent on May 2, 1955. The empties were to be left at Sargent for use by the scrapping constractor to haul out the rail being removed from the line. D&RGW No. 483 was on the head end as the train rounded the reverse curve just above Shirley. The photograph was shot from the cupola of caboose No. 0574, which was located directly behind helper engine No. 489.**

**SHIRLEY** (originally named Silver Creek) — Milepost 228.3, Elevation 8,669 feet, 13 miles from Salida — was reached only a week later. Shirley quickly became a booming railroad camp, but it was the "end of track" (or "front") only briefly. However, tracklaying was temporarily stalled at Shirley due to a lack of rail — although grading proceeded without delay. The route over the Divide began its serious climb at this point, with the summit only 12 miles away by rail, and nearly 2,200 feet higher. Although the ruling 4.0-percent grade remained the same, the route began its area of maximum curvature here — which would not end until Buxton was reached, near the western foot of Marshall Pass. The

D&RG allowed eight tents containing saloons and dancehalls to be erected at Shirley. Besides these "hell-town" tents, a half-dozen business and construction-camp tents were thrown up adjacent to the siding.

After the D&RG reached Shirley, Sanderson stagecoaches began meeting the daily passenger train. However, there was so much traffic by train that some railroad patrons had to layover a night in the rough-hewn construction camp. And the jolting journey by stage over the pass was hardly what one could call a pleasant ride. Never-the-less, as many as three or four stagecoaches were required to carry the railroad passengers on to Gunnison and beyond.

*(Continued on Page 55)*

**D&RG STATION MAP OF SHIRLEY — 1889**    *Shirley.*

GEORGE E. MELLEN PHOTO – RICHARD A. RONZIO COLLECTION

OPPOSITE (above): On the grade to Marshall Pass, this long freight train of the 1880's had stopped at Shirley to take on water. Helper engine No. 276 was outfitted with link-and-pin coupler pockets, suitable for working in switching service on dual-gauge trackage. An enclosure constructed around the base of the water tank helped keep water from freezing in sub-zero winter weather. During about the same period (below), the Denver & Rio Grande's caboose No. 0580 was adorned with bunting for some unknown reason — as it waited at the end of a long train during the mid-1880's.

ABOVE: In this photograph, taken after the contractor had abandoned Shirley as a construction camp, little remained of the once bustling community. The camp's former main street headed west; however, when this scene was photographed, it was just a part of the Marshall Pass wagon road. Poncha Creek was still meandering through the area, and piles of crossties were still stacked along the stream bank. Crossing the hillside, directly above the campsite, the D&RG mainline ran in the opposite direction, en route to the summit of Marshall Pass. The steepness of the grade is easily discernible in this view.

47

**THE END WAS NEAR** as May 24, 1955, rolled around. A trainload of scrap rail — pulled up from Gunnison-area lines — drifted downgrade past the curve west of Shirley, heading for Salida. The engine is No. 483, while the gondolas are some of the ones that were hauled to Sargent, shown in the view on Page 45.

THE RENOWNED W. H. JACKSON positioned himself near the wye at Shirley for this D&RG publicity shot of a three-locomotive freight train climbing toward Marshall Pass. This was after most of Shirley's temporary residents had moved on to "greener pastures." And notice that one of the turnouts had been disconnected at the Shirley wye in favor of locomotive turn-arounds taking place elsewhere on the line.

W. H. JACKSON PHOTO – COLORADO RAILROAD MUSEUM COLLECTION

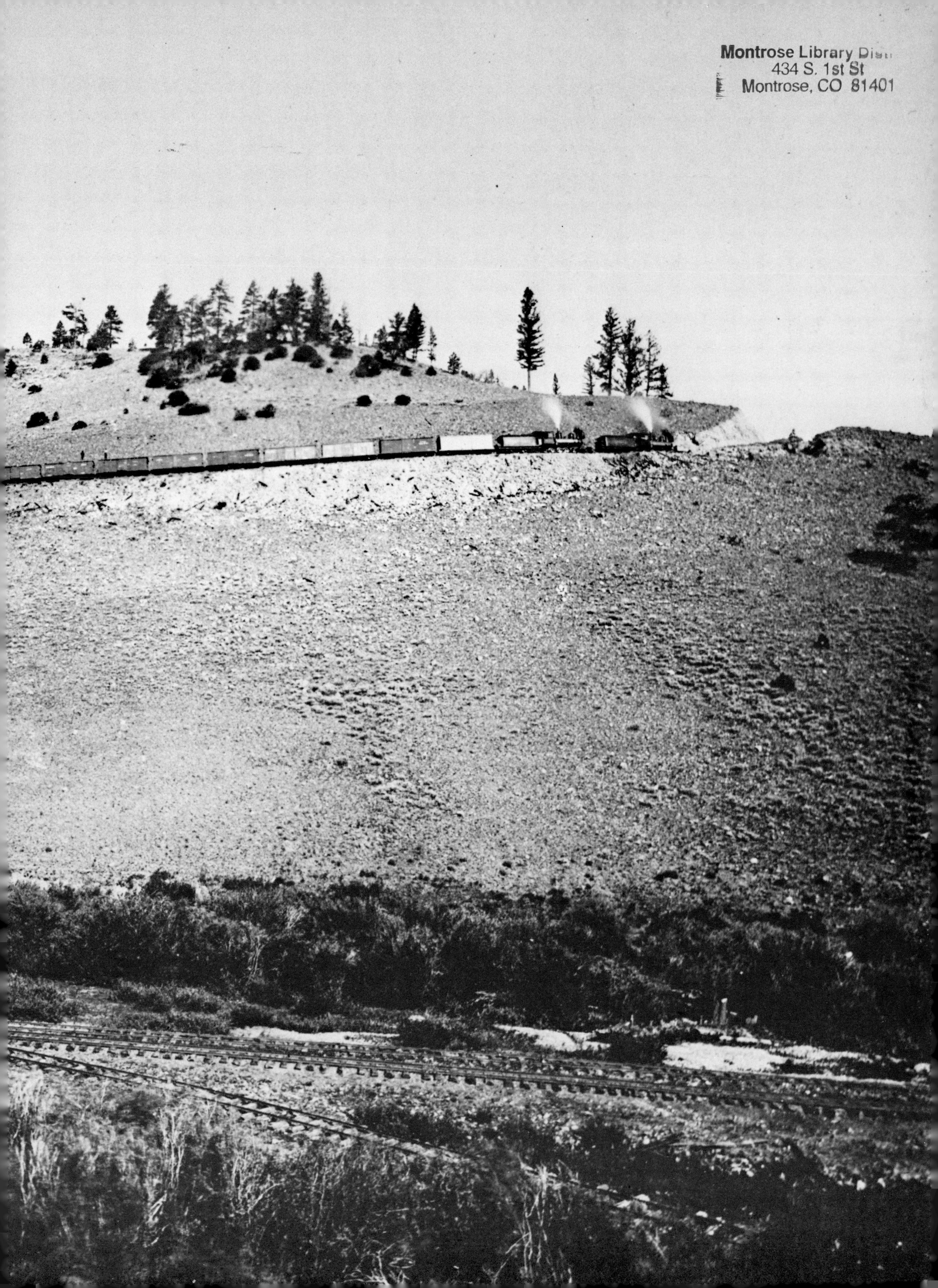

**MOUNT OURAY** — on the right-hand page — could be considered the main obstacle encountered by the survey crew laying-out the route over Marshall Pass. D&RG track wound upgrade, gaining altitude as it was carved out along the flanks of the peak. (Refer to the drawing on Page 6.) The photographer's special train occupied the siding at Shirley, and was headed westbound. Ruins of the settlement are visible on the side of the hill. Stacks of ties had been stored beside the passing siding. The Shirley loop and bridge show up at the far left.

DETROIT PUBLISHING CO

1002 SHIRLEY GUNNISON DIVIDE RG RY

A HELPER LOCOMOTIVE was posed for W. H. Jackson one summer day in 1881, along the grade above Shirley. The water tank, depot and a separate freight house are visible on the right-hand page. Tents — some with false fronts — make up the majority of the structures. Supply wagons and dray animals can be seen off to the side of Shirley's main street. The railroad buildings along the track are: a bunkhouse, section house, water tank, passenger depot and freighthouse.

54

Before the construction outfit of Green & Foody moved out of Shirley, a small depot was built across the track from the water tank, and several more independent "tent buildings" were put up. Of course, saloons outnumbered all other establishments. However, the contractor started laying rail up the grade west of Shirley before the end of May, 1881, and the handwriting was on the wall for this construction camp. There was also a short spur to the Rawley mine and mill, the only major mining activity on either side of the pass.

The three stations between Shirley and the Continental Divide were little more than passing sidings. They were as follows:

*(Continued on Page 66)*

631. MARSHALL PASS, FROM ABOVE SHIRLEY.

SHIRLEY WAS LOCATED directly below the seated gentleman in the view taken during 1881. Smoke lingered in the gulch far below, obscuring the valley floor. A large number of small rock cuts — like the one in this scene — were necessary along the route over Marshall Pass. This view was taken looking up the scenic valley of Poncha Creek.

OPPOSITE: As a helper engine paused on its return from assisting a train up Marshall Pass, the photographer posed the crew for an interesting period picture. Mears Junction appears on the distant valley floor.

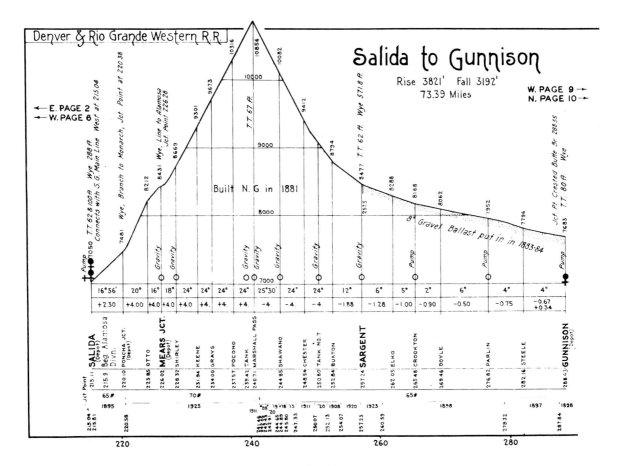

903. VIEW FROM NEAR SHIRLEY

03257 ON MARSHALL PASS ABOVE MEARS

W. H. JACKSON PHOTO – RICHARD A RONZIO COLLECTION

DURING JUNE OF 1884, Major Shadrach K. Hooper, the D&RG's general passenger and ticket agent, provided the photographer with this oversize sleeping car — according to Jackson Thode, former D&RGW official. The car was equipped with a large observation platform, nearly filled with passengers. It is sup-

posed that family members and/or friends accompanied William H. Jackson on this trip over Marshall Pass (as was often the case on the famous photographer's journeys by rail). The entourage was viewed as the camera was pointed toward the north at Mears Junction. Locomotive No. 273 was a Class 60 2–8–0, a

58

Baldwin product of 1882 (later reclassified as a C-16). It is interesting to note the bay window on the observation platform, which provided enjoyment for the passengers riding this luxurious car. Another Jackson view of this unusual car exists, taken on the Silverton Branch during this photographic excursion.

**KEENE AT MILEPOST 232**

THIS GROUPING of photographs was taken on the zig-zag loops above Shirley. Brakemen "decorated" the tops of cars, while the train descended Marshall Pass in 1882. Before the advent of the airbrake, No. 273 could not hold back this mixed freight and passenger train without assistance from the brakemen. In the upper view, scrap rail from the Gunnison area was being transported to Salida, May 24, 1955. Farther up Marshall Pass, near the summit, a passenger train of 1882 vintage was posed above a three-locomotive freight train on a lower loop of track. Notice the old "turtle-roofed" cars at the head end of the train.

W. H. JACKSON PHOTO – JACKSON C. THODE COLLECTION

**A FEW MONTHS EARLIER**, the photographer captured this view of construction taking place at the same site as shown previously (on Page 61). A rail-and-tie train, had locomotives at each end, facing in both directions, in order to have one engine facing down the grade. The engine tenders were notorious for derailing when backing downgrade on such rough trackage. Apparently, the track gang was adding "ballast" — rocks and dirt from along the grade — to help stabilize the rather primitive trackage. Notice the crude hand-hewn crossties.

DELL A. McCOY PHOTO

ONE OF THE FIRST large cuts above Shirley appears in this color view, taken on the old railroad grade to Marshall Pass in 1990 — during the last days of a glorious Colorado summer — in September.

E. G. MORRISON'S MOUNTAIN VIEWS – RICHARD A RONZIO COLLECTION

THIS SWEEPING CURVE, near Milepost 231.6, provided a view of Mount Ouray for the enjoyment of train passengers. A short freight of 1882 vintage — with five boxcars and a four-wheel caboose in tow — was headed upgrade over newly placed rough-hewn crossties. The D&RG used good judgment in grading the line with super-elevated curves.

**A ROTARY SNOWPLOW** was pressed into service to clear snowdrifts from the Marshall Pass line, as shown in this wintry scene. This view was photographed on Marshall Pass sometime before 1903. Two diamond-stacked locomotives provided the power, and the caboose carried brakemen and a conductor, and extra men to help shovel-out problem drifts or snowslides. In the lower photograph, taken during the same time period, westbound passenger train No. 65 was heading for Gunnison as darkness closed in. The train required a helper on the point because of snow on the track. On the next page, a 2–8–0 helper crossed over the trestle above Ouray Creek, about three miles east of Marshall Pass. This location is a fill today, as shown on Page 72.

**POCONO SPUR AT MILEPOST 237.6**

THE TIMBER TRESTLE over Ouray Creek had been filled-in by the time this photograph was taken sometime prior to 1903. Link-and-pin couplers were still in use, as westbound D&RG Train 65 — with a helper on the head end — cleared a short snowshed. A rock retaining wall helped support the grade, so that rain water would not wash away the earth fill. The train consisted of five cars, with an RPO car and an express/baggage car directly behind the locomotives. Incidentally, the D&RG constructed a number of snowsheds in narrow rock cuts on this route, primarily to prevent blowing snow from filling-in the cuts.

DELL A. McCOY PHOTO

OPPOSITE: Photographed during the September autumn-color extravaganza of 1990, it seems as though this view is at the same location as the picture shown on this page. The photographer was looking downgrade.

OPPOSITE: The top of Marshall Pass was reached by tracklayers in 1881, and the three views on Pages 74–75 were taken shortly thereafter. Tents of the construction-contractor's camp were still in place, as seen in the two upper photographs, adjacent to the new wooden-frame depot. In the lower view, a westbound passenger train had halted at the summit depot. The train was headed by one of the D&RG's small 2-6-0's (probably one of the 1876 Baldwin Moguls), followed by two turtle-roofed baggage/mail cars. The Marshall Pass station was built on a sharp curve at the end of a rock cut. These photographs were obviously all taken prior to the construction of the snowsheds. The smaller of the two tents adjacent to the depot carried a saloon sign, and a woman was standing in the doorway. Antora Mountain, at an elevation of 13,266 feet, was south of the pass, and formed the backdrop above. Gondolas used for ballast work and a supply car occupied the track in this view looking toward the west.

**MARSHALL PASS** — Milepost 240.7, Elevation 10,856 feet, with a capacity to hold 120 cars — was the highest point the D&RG had reached up to this time, 47.7 miles east of Gunnison. The crest of the pass was notable for an unusual tangent (straight) track, about three-quarters of a mile long on the eastern side of the Great Divide. Just above the tangent, the mainline curved sharply to the south, and then reversed itself on an even-sharper curve right at the summit. A water tank was constructed near the upper end of the straightaway — to take advantage of the water of the creek at the

*(Continued on Page 86)*

**OPPOSITE:** The Denver & Rio Grande constructed a short snowshed on the first curve above the water tank atop Marshall Pass, as reproduced in the views on this page and two pictures on Page 77. Mount Ouray rises to 13,971 feet above sea level and provides a magnificent backdrop for this 1881 view of the newly-completed snowshed. Outfit cars were on a spur to the left of the snowshed.

**ON THIS PAGE,** the photographer made two separate shots a year or two later, which show the construction camp at the pass, made up of log dwellings with sod roofs. D&RG No. 406 was a new Class 70 2–8–0 (subsequently reclassified as a C-19), used at first as a helper engine. This engine became No. 346, and it is now on display at the Colorado Railroad Museum in Golden.

DENVER & RIO GRANDE R.R.

SCENIC LINE
OF THE
WORLD

1887 – 1922

**OPPOSITE: An eastbound stock-train movement out of Gunnison was photographed on the long tangent at Marshall Pass on May 2, 1955. The snow-capped Sangre de Cristo Range looms high on the horizon. The lower color view, taken on the same date, is of the last eastbound D&RGW train at Marshall Pass. Jack Thode — hands in his pockets at this chilly elevation — supervised the proceedings as one of the railroad officials on this sad occasion. Looking toward the west in the view below, the foreground buildings (left to right) were: a section house, a coalshed (beside the track) and a bunkhouse, not to mention outhouses. The long curving snowshed crossed the actual point of the Great Divide, where the eastern and western watersheds separate — with the one on the west dividing toward Gunnison and the Pacific Ocean, and the one on the east dividing toward Salida and the Atlantic Ocean.**

**HEADED FOR GUNNISON** on September 6, 1947, the Rocky Mountain Railroad Club's five-car excursion train of that date was approaching the Marshall Pass snowshed. The train consisted of an open-door baggage car, with "bull" boards (to protect passengers), three coaches, and the parlor car "Chama," with D&RGW No. 494 on the point. Below, the Marshall Pass station sign was attached to the side of one of the section houses at the summit.

OTTO C. PERRY PHOTO – RICHARD A. RONZIO COLLECTION

**HERE ARE TWO VIEWS** of the same locomotive — No. 489 — on two separate occasions. No. 489 was emerging from the east portal of the Marshall Pass snowshed in both of these views — taken two years apart. Antora Mountain, directly south of the snowshed, appears on the horizon — with snowfences situated to block drifting snow. The photograph (above) was taken on October 9, 1953, as a livestock train was en route to Salida, while (below) a dismantling train was drifting out of the east portal of the snowshed during September of 1955.

JOHN KRAUSE PHOTO – COLORADO RAILROAD MUSEUM COLLECTION

**FRAMED IN THE EAST END** of the Marshall Pass snowshed, D&RGW No. 489 is shown after helping the last train from Salida to the summit on May 2, 1955. In the upper view (next page), the locomotive was being turned inside the shed and headed back downgrade to Salida. The lower photograph was taken facing toward the north, at Marshall Pass and shows almost the entire snowshed — with the horseshoe-curved section containing the depot and turntable being in the middle of the picture. A mine structure is in the distant background (far left), just above the western end of the snowshed. The line to Salida heads downhill and out of the view to the right. The snowshed below the cut emerged out of it to the right. The grade dropping to Sargent is discernable at the far right.

84

**LOOKING SOUTH into the open end of the horseshoe curve across the summit of Marshall Pass in 1889, the massive bulk of Antora Mountain towered in the distance. The rounded section of the snowshed, which covered the turntable, was directly below Antora's summit.**

were two additional bunkhouses for workers.

A landmark at the western end of the snowshed was a lookout tower. Atop this tall tower observers could view approximately six miles down the western slope of the pass. The right-of-way contorted downgrade over no less than five terraces, allowing the track to drop some 1,444 feet past Shawano to a station called Chester. Over 16 miless of mainline track were required to cover this rugged mountainous terrain.

*(Continued on Page 104)*

**THE MARSHALL PASS SNOWSHED** appears in this color view, as the photographer aimed his camera toward the northwest. Structures from left to right are: a bunkhouse, the depot, the turntable section of the shed, and leading off to the right, the west end of the shed.

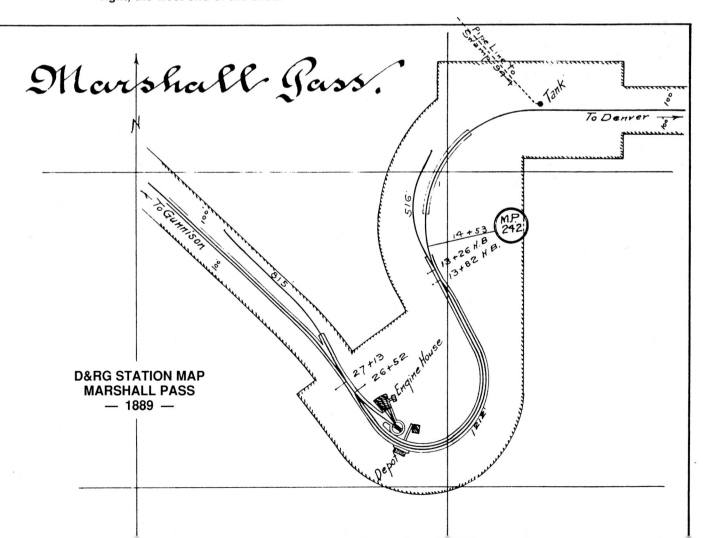

*Marshall Pass.*

N

Pipe Line to Swamp 954+

Tank

To Denver

100
100

516'

14+53
13+26 H.B.
13+82 H.B.

M.P. 242

To Gunnison
100
100

815'

1812'

27+13
26+52

Engine House

Depot

**D&RG STATION MAP
MARSHALL PASS
— 1889 —**

**ONE OF THE HIGHLIGHTS** of a trip over Marshall Pass was to climb the stairway at the lookout tower for the magnificent view provided from the top of the Continental Divide. The enlargement below (left) gives you a better look at the tower and the exterior of the three- stall enginehouse — part of the snowshed — with the adjacent covered turntable. Below (right), this view provides you with a look at the interior of the snow- shed, before the outside sheathing and roof were added.

IT WAS NOT AN EASY TASK to photograph the interior of the dark snowshed on Marshall Pass, but the results were well worth the effort — as shown in these two photographs. The turntable was used to reverse the direction of helper locomotives so they could return downgrade on either side of the pass. This view was photographed on August 30, 1947. It was not un-usual for a train to have two helpers for the 4.0-percent grade. In the lower view, No. 499 — which was being used on the Rocky Mountain Railroad Club excursion of September 6, 1947 — stood on the siding (headed westbound), with the turntable lead track in view at left.

RICHARD H. KINDIG PHOTO

**INSIDE THE SNOWSHED** at Marshall Pass, shafts of sunlight furnished the only available light for the dark interior, shown here as photographed on May 2, 1955. The upper view (at the top of the next page) shows salvage-train workers removing rail in the shed during the fall of 1955. A study of shed construction reveals the simplicity of design. At the west portal a freight train had stopped on the mainline after arriving from Gunnison. An 800-foot spur track, which had its own portal (separate from the snowshed's main west portal during the 1880's) leads off to the right.

**AS PHOTOGRAPHED** on September 18, 1948, the roof construction of the snowshed appears simple in this view atop Marshall Pass. Side bracing was required because of the high winds and heavy snows at this 10,856-foot elevation.

ELMORE FREDERICK COLLECTION

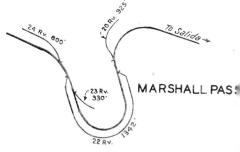

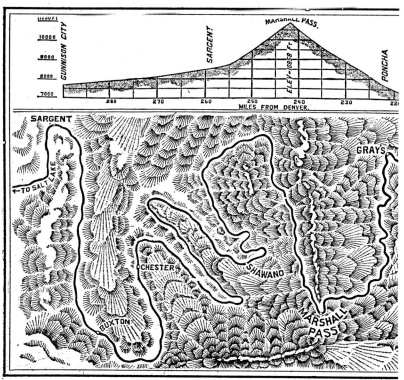

TWO GOOD VIEWS of the west end of the Marshall Pass snowshed appear on these pages — with the model builder in mind. The upper photograph shows the tail end of an eastbound livestock train as it entered the shed, powered by three K-37's, Numbers 490, 491 and 498, on September 30, 1939. The "doghouse" located on the rear of the tender provided shelter for head-end brakemen. The doghouse was steam-heated and provided a warm shelter from which the brakemen could watch the cars in the train. It appears that No. 498 had not consumed much of the coal that was taken-on at Sargent for the climb up Marshall Pass. In the lower view (at right), ventilators are visible on top of the Marshall Pass snowshed roof, and there seem to be openings along the upper walls for additional ventilation. Notice the side-bracing, which had been constructed to protect the shed from the strong winds that sometimes blow across the top of the Divide in excess of 100 mph.

BELOW: The Rocky Mountain Railroad Club excursion on September 6, 1947, had crossed the Continental Divide inside the snowshed, and it was now heading downgrade toward Gunnison.

RICHARD H. KINDIG PHOTO – ELMORE FREDERICK COLLECTION

OTTO C. PERRY PHOTO – RICHARD A. RONZIO COLLECTION

OTTO C. PERRY
DENVER, COLO.

THE PHOTOGRAPHER POSED for his own camera on this memorable expedition over Marshall Pass, August 13, 1955. On this occasion, a Fairmont section car was making the last trip over the pass before the dismantling train began to work its way out of Sargent. To the left of the steaming "pop car" radiator is a glimpse of the water tank at Shawano. This scene was photographed just outside the west portal of the snowshed.

THIS VERY EARLY PICTURE was photographed atop Marshall Pass, and it offers a view of the distant grade that circled around a low hill before it reached the tank at Shawano. Much of the snowshed probably had been cut from timber in the surrounding forest land. It appears that the logs in the foreground were full-grown trees, which had been blown over during some previous gale.

THE FINAL EASTBOUND FREIGHT movement over Marshall Pass was on the afternoon of May 1955. All remaining stock cars were assembled in Sargent, and the last run over the pass began with a bulldozer on a flatcar, approximately 30 empty stock cars and two cabooses. Engine 489 was on the head end, and helper No. 483 was coupled-in just ahead of the cabooses. In the upper view, the train was approaching the west portal of the snowshed. In the background of the lower scene, the steep slopes of 13,855-foot Antora Mountain are still blanketed with deep snow in early May. The two cabooses on the rear end were for a select group of railfan photographers for this last eastbound D&RGW train over this legendary pass.

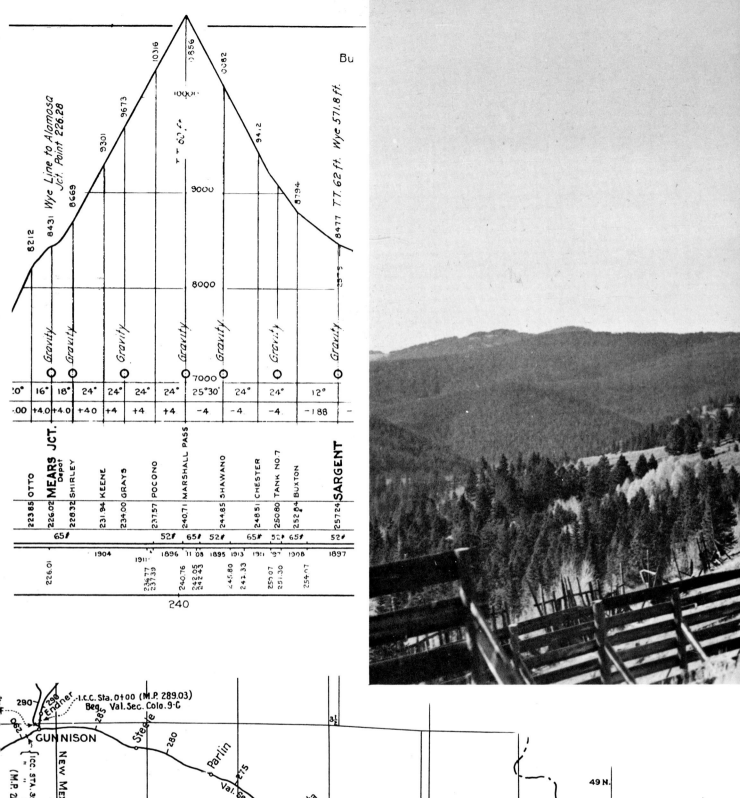

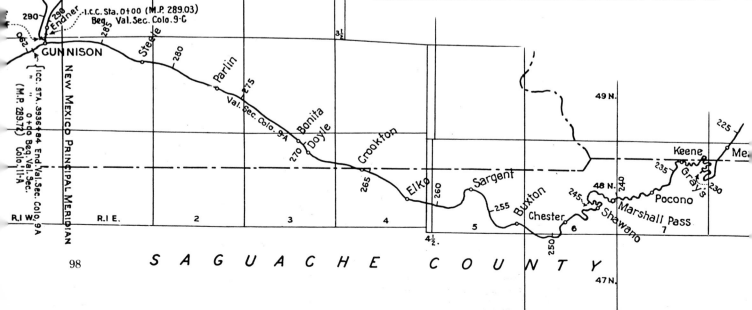

**D&RG STATION MAP**
**HILDEN – 1889**
(Siding No. 7 in 1882 timetable)

**FOUR LOCOMOTIVES** were required to haul the live-stock train of October 9, 1953, up the grade out of Sargent. The engines were Numbers 489, 483, 480 and 482, all K-37 2-8-2's, shown here near the top of Marshall Pass.

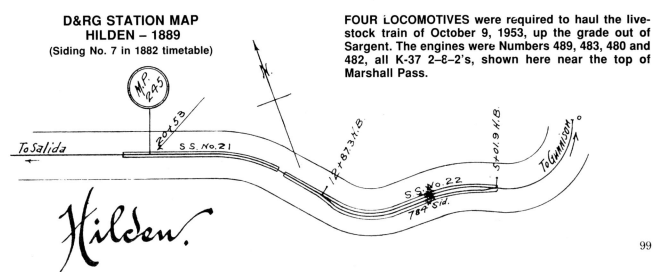

99

E. J. HALEY PHOTO

THE SNOWY WEST SLOPE of Antora Mountain came Into view as the last D&RGW train of empty stock cars worked upgrade over Marshall Pass — above Chester — on May 2, 1955.

BELOW: Looking down on the Shawano tank, a long freight train was in view as it climbed the loops up to Marshall Pass, about 1885. The grade in view between the train and Shawano was Otto Mears' toll road over Marshall Pass, built in 1878–1879, and sold to the Rio Grande for $13,000 in 1880. The photographer of this lower view is unknown.

RICHARD A. RONZIO COLLECTION

HAULING COAL, these gondolas were on the grade below Marshall Pass. The coal came from mines in the Crested Butte area and Baldwin district. These mines annually shipped thousands of carloads of coal over the pass, providing the D&RGW with much of its tonnage on this route. A helper locomotive was in service on the rear end of this coal drag. An early-day passenger train out of Gunnison is shown here as it climbed the grade above Shawano prior to 1893. It is remarkable how many heavy passenger cars these comparitively small locomotives could pul on the 4.0-percent grade. In all likelihood, this passenger train was Train 8, the "Atlantic Express," en route from Salt Lake City to Denver. This was the only eastbound passenger train due at Shawano during the morning — at 9:18 a.m. The engine probably was a Class 60 200-series 2–8–0.

ROBERT W. RICHARDSON PHOTO – COLORADO RAILROAD MUSEUM

**ABOVE: During 1955, the dismantling train had reached Shawano, while — below — locomotives 492, 499 and 490, at the rear of the train, were at Shawano on September 3, 1939. The photograph was taken from the rear platform of Train 315, the "Shavano."**

RICHARD H. KINDIG PHOTO

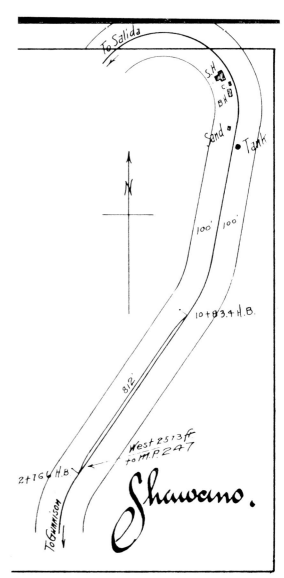

**SHAWANO** — Milepost 244.8, Elevation 10,082 feet — was the location of a water tank.

ROBERT W. RICHARDSON PHOTO – COLORADO RAILROAD MUSEUM

HAULING COAL, these gondolas were on the grade below Marshall Pass. The coal came from mines in the Crested Butte area and Baldwin district. These mines annually shipped thousands of carloads of coal over the pass, providing the D&RGW with much of its tonnage on this route. A helper locomotive was in service on the rear end of this coal drag. An early-day passenger train out of Gunnison is shown here as it climbed the grade above Shawano prior to 1893. It is remarkable how many heavy passenger cars these comparitively small locomotives could pul on the 4.0-percent grade. In all likelihood, this passenger train was Train 8, the "Atlantic Express," en route from Salt Lake City to Denver. This was the only eastbound passenger train due at Shawano during the morning — at 9:18 a.m. The engine probably was a Class 60 200-series 2-8-0.

W. H. JACKSON PHOTO – E. J. HALEY COLLECTION

MARSHALL PASS.

SOMEWHERE HIGH on the heavily timbered west slope of Marshall Pass, William H. Jackson photographed the construction of the D&RG in 1881. This location was close to the summit. Engine No. 41 was an 1880 Class 60 2–8–0, named the "Grand Cañon" — renumbered "229" in 1884. This photograph probably was taken on the same day in 1881 as the one on this page. The lady and gentleman standing beside the engineer are obviously the same couple in both views. Otto Mears' toll road crosses the hillside in the background. The train (above) was climbing around a second hairpin loop above Shawano. The Shawano water tank appears in the scene just in front of the headlight of No. 41 — which was hauling a string of empty rail and tie cars. At right, near Milepost 243, Robert W. Richardson of the Colorado Railroad Museum believes this was the site of a major runaway train wreck the Rio Grande suffered during early-day operations.

**ABOVE: During 1955, the dismantling train had reached Shawano, while — below — locomotives 492, 499 and 490, at the rear of the train, were at Shawano on September 3, 1939. The photograph was taken from the rear platform of Train 315, the "Shavano."**

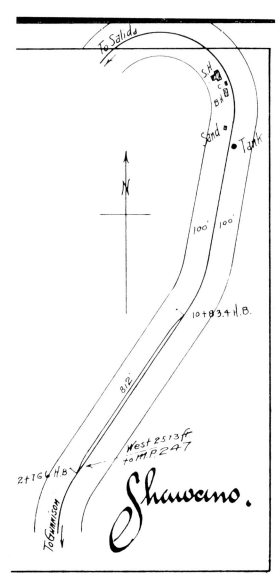

**SHAWANO** — Milepost 244.8, Elevation 10,082 feet — was the location of a water tank.

**D&RGW ENGINE NO. 483** was leading the last train into Shawano, as seen in this picture taken from the roof of Caboose 0574. Both engines on this train took on water at Shawano tank. The rear of the same train was photographed while at the tank, with the scenic backdrop of Chipeta Mountain, 12,853 feet above sea level (at left) and Mount Ouray, at an elevation of 13,971 feet. (Chipeta, of course, was the wife of Chief Ouray.)

**THE LONG SNOWSHEDS below Marshall Pass lasted for only a few years after construction — until hot cinders from passing engines burned them down, or they were considered too dangerous to leave standing. The tank at Shawano appears in all three views. A long freight had just passed through the longer shed in the upper picture at the right, and it reached the summit a short time later. The old Mears toll road also shows up well, crossing the middle of the upper photograph.**

**HILDEN** — Milepost 245.3, Elevation 10,301 feet — was originally called Siding Number Seven. Snowshed No. 22 originally covered both the 784-foot siding and the mainline at this location. Snowshed No. 21 was just above Hilden, with only a short open section of track between the two sheds.

*(Continued on Page 110)*

**SHAWANO TANK** was always an important water stop on the long climb up the west side of Marshall Pass. The original tank was built in 1881 across the track from this one and against the mountainside. The tank's original location is shown in the lower left view. two upper photographs were taken below Shawano from the caboose during the trip made on May 2, 1955. The D&RG's "Shoshone," No. 402 — a Class 70 (C-19)

2–8–0, built in 1881 — had stopped at the Shawano section house, with the water tank just behind the caboose. The first two cars are two different versions of the railroad's early refrigerator cars. At the top left, the last train was climbing the grade between Chester and Shawano — and below, the dismantling crew was ripping up the rails at Shawano,

**DESCENDING THE GRADE** below Shawano, D&RG No. 285 was posed in 1884 for a publicity shot. This 2–8–0 was a Class 60 built by Baldwin in 1882. The large original glass negative included the top of Marshall Pass. One of the very early turtle-roof baggage-and-express cars — No. 150 — and possibly what was locomotive No. 86 were photographed near the summit of Marshall Pass in 1884. In the lower view on the next page, a Rocky Mountain Railroad Club excursion train was near Chester — which may have been called Mill Switch curve. The train was dropping downgrade en route to Sargent, with No. 494 on the point. This run was photographed during September of 1948.

**CHESTER** — Milepost 248.5, Elevation 9,412 feet — was mainly a passing siding (1,184 feet long), with a 28-car capacity. Chester was 39.9 miles east of Gunnison, half way down the line to Sargent, just west of the 4.0-percent grade to the summit. Incidentally, Shawano (usually spelled "Shavano") was the name of a Ute Indian chieftan, a name also given to the railroad's Salida–Gunnison–Montrose passenger train. The so-called Shawano Loop was a scenic attraction of the climb up the western side of Marshall Pass. Not only did this loop give tourists a feeling of reversing directions, but it also allowed them to look down the twisting grade the train had just passed over.

110

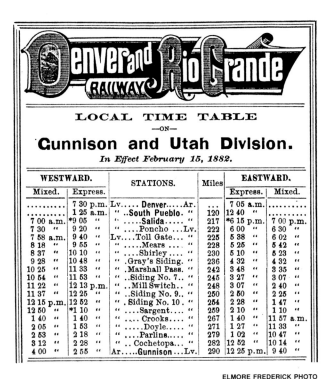

# Denver and Rio Grande
## RAILWAY

### LOCAL TIME TABLE
—ON—
### Gunnison and Utah Division.
*In Effect February 15, 1882.*

| WESTWARD. | | STATIONS. | Miles | EASTWARD. | |
|---|---|---|---|---|---|
| Mixed. | Express. | | | Express. | Mixed. |
| ......... | 7 30 p.m. | Lv.....Denver.....Ar. | ... | 7 05 a.m. | ......... |
| ......... | 1 25 a.m. | " ..South Pueblo. " | 120 | 12 40 " | ......... |
| 7 00 a.m. | *9 05 " | " .....Salida.... " | 217 | *6 15 p.m. | 7 00 p.m. |
| 7 30 " | 9 20 " | " ....Poncho ...Lv. | 222 | 6 00 " | 6 30 " |
| 7 58 a.m. | 9 40 " | Lv....Toll Gate... " | 225 | 5 38 " | 6 02 " |
| 8 18 " | 9 55 " | " .....Mears .... " | 228 | 5 25 " | 5 42 " |
| 8 37 " | 10 10 " | " ....Shirley.... " | 230 | 5 10 " | 5 23 " |
| 9 28 " | 10 48 " | " .Gray's Siding. " | 236 | 4 32 " | 4 32 " |
| 10 25 " | 11 33 " | " .Marshall Pass. " | 242 | 3 48 " | 3 35 " |
| 10 54 " | 11 53 " | " ..Siding No. 7.. " | 245 | 3 27 " | 3 07 " |
| 11 22 " | 12 13 p.m. | " ..Mill Switch.. " | 248 | 3 07 " | 2 40 " |
| 11 37 " | 12 25 " | " ..Siding No. 9.. " | 250 | 2 50 " | 2 25 " |
| 12 15 p.m. | 12 52 " | " .Siding No. 10. " | 254 | 2 28 " | 1 47 " |
| 12 50 " | *1 10 " | " ....Sargent.... " | 259 | 2 10 " | 1 10 " |
| 1 40 " | 1 40 " | " .....Crooks.... " | 267 | 1 40 " | 11 57 a.m. |
| 2 05 " | 1 53 " | " .....Doyle..... " | 271 | 1 27 " | 11 33 " |
| 2 53 " | 2 18 " | " ....Parlins.... " | 279 | 1 02 " | 10 47 " |
| 3 12 " | 2 28 " | " ..Cochetopa.. " | 282 | 12 52 " | 10 14 " |
| 4 00 " | 2 55 " | Ar.....Gunnison...Lv. | 290 | 12 25 p.m. | 9 40 " |

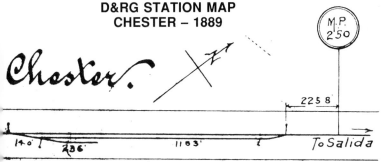

## D&RG STATION MAP
## CHESTER – 1889

M.P. 250

Chester.

225 8

140'   236'   1163'   To Salida

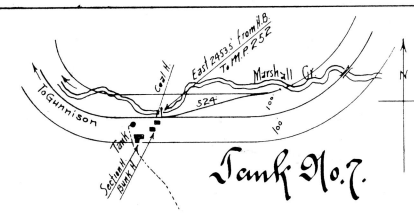

*Tank No. 7.*

**THE LAST TRAIN** over Marshall Pass — a long string of empties — rattled past Tank No. 7 on May 2, 1955. Although winter had not yet relaxed its icy grip, and the tank supports were still heavily encrusted with ice from water leakage, the first blush of spring had restored some color to the foliage along the bed of Marshall Creek.

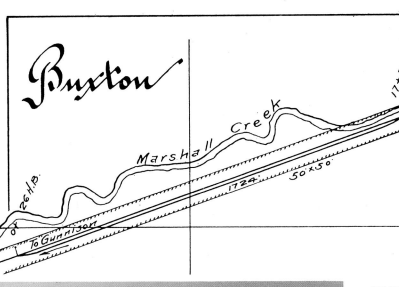

*Buxton*

**STATION MAPS OF BUXTON AND TANK SEVEN
ON THE D&RG – 1889**

**JUST EAST OF SARGENT,** the same train shown above, began its climb through the sagebrush-covered hills just east of this helper station — as the train worked its way up the easy 1.88-percent grade on the four and one-half miles to Buxton.

E. J. HALEY PHOTO

**TANK NUMBER SEVEN** — Milepost 250.8. West of Chester, the mainline descended nearly two miles to Tank Number Seven, about seven miles east of Sargent.
**BUXTON** — Milepost 252.8, Elevation 8,794 feet — was a passing siding with a 43-car capacity. From Buxton, it was about five miles downgrade to Sargent. However, there was a station called **Jackson Spur** between Buxton and Sargent, not listed in later timetables. All the way from Mears Junction to Sargent, the D&RG stations virtually had only one purpose, to serve the needs of the railroad as trains toiled over Marshall Pass.

113

**THE LAST FOUR-ENGINE livestock train to leave Sargent for Marshall Pass was photographed on October 9, 1953. This same train was photographed again later in the day, as it neared the top of the pass. See Page 99.**

**SARGENT** (properly spelled "Sargent," *without* an "s" following the "t") — Milepost 257.2, Elevation 8,477 feet — was named for one Joseph Sargent, a pioneer innkeeper in the area. The settlement was originally called **Marshalltown**, in honor of Lieutenant William L. Marshall, the young U.S. Corps of Engineers officer who was the first American surveyor to cross the pass that now bears his name. (Lieutenant Marshall was part of the Wheeler Survey, which had been working in southwestern Colorado in 1873. He trekked across the unnamed pass en route to Denver during the late fall of that year, attempting to save time on his journey because he was suffering from a toothache.)

Sargent was the primary Rio Grande station on the west side of the pass, even as Mears Junction was more-or-less its counterpart on the east side. Besides having a water tank, wooden single-story depot and a siding capacity of over 150 cars (which had been reduced to 100 by 1949), this location on the railroad was principally a helper station. Helper engines were routinely assigned to trains climbing the pass — which went from less than a 2.0-percent gradient at Sargent to a stiff 4.0-percent near Buxton.

Adjacent to the depot, water tank and passing track at Sargent was a six-stall roundhouse, with a 62-foot turntable. All of these facilities were situated inside a wye — all of which was in a bow of Marshall Creek. (The "tail" of the wye crossed the creek on a low pile trestle, Bridge 257-A.)

Early on, the railroad built a large coaling trestle along the mainline east of the wye and roundhouse. This facility was equipped with gravity-fed coal chutes, and it was a rather imposing structure. Across the tracks from the coaling trestle there were livestock pens, and several smaller railroad buildings were situated west of the wye, including a combination section-car and tool shed, a section house, bunkhouse and an eating house, as well as other minor structures.

Beyond Sargent, the Gunnison Extension still had a little over 31 miles to traverse before reaching Gunnison, most of which more-or-less paralleled Tomichi Creek in the valley of the same name. En route, there were five passing sidings; however, none of these stations had settlements except for Parlin — and this small community could hardly be called a "town." The stations between Sargent and Gunnison were as follows:

*(Continued on Page 133)*

OTTO C. PERRY PHOTO

**K-28 NO. 474 AND K-37 NO. 492 — both outside-frame Mikados — double-headed a 23-car freight train eastbound out of Sargent, en route to Marshall Pass and Salida. In this view taken during October of 1941, smoke from another 2–8–2, No. 493, can be seen back in the yard, at the rear of the train.**

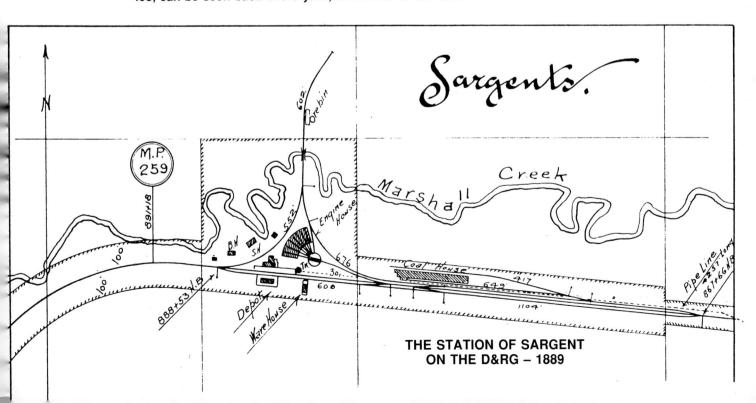

**THE STATION OF SARGENT
ON THE D&RG – 1889**

**THE COALING FACILITY** at Sargent was an impressive structure, constructed to fuel D&RG locomotives for the tough climb up Marshall Pass — and down the other slope to Salida. The railroad called this facility a "locomotive-incline coaling station," built for dump-bottom coal cars (namely, National Dump gondolas in both the 700 and 800 series, as well as Ingoldsby dump cars in the 900 series). These views were taken on September 20, 1952, as No. 483 shoved a string of National Dump cars up the trestle to the coal bunkers, where she retrieved two empties, as shown at the lower left. The two loads were then taken back up to the top and spotted over the bunkers. (The Sargent coaling station had four coal chutes, each with a 100-ton capacity.) Below, a Rocky Mountain Railroad Club excursion train had arrived at Sargent for a water stop. The business section of the town and residential houses are on the left (or south) of the little combination passenger-freight depot. This photograph was taken from on top of the coal trestle.

ON MARCH 31, 1955, the D&RGW's impressive coaling station could still be photographed — a short time before the wrecking crew came along during the fall of that year. Notice on the lower-left view an 1880's- type stub switch (or turnout) still in use. The view at lower right shows the coal-chute aprons that hinged down onto the tender for a delivery guideway.

**A FAREWELL GLIMPSE OF SARGENT** was had from the rear caboose platform of the last eastbound freight train, headed for Salida on the afternoon of May 2, 1955. The photographer snapped this view as he looked west, down the mainline, which led to Gunnison. Soon, the dismantlers descended upon this trackage to rip up the rails that served so long and so well. The Sargent depot is behind the water tank, and many other railroad structures are scattered about the wye and yard. The sandhouse and sandbin can be seen at the right. This historic last train was headed for Marshall Pass and on to Salida.

**D&RGW 2–8–2 NO. 494** was resting on the Sargent turntable on August 14, 1939, with "extra" flags flying. The engine was waiting to help boost the next eastbound freight up the steep grade to the summit of Marshall Pass.

D. E. ROGERS PHOTO – SUNDANCE COLLECTION

**D&RGW ENGINE 480** (above) was approaching the sandhouse at Sargent on October 6, 1954. The structure to the left had a coal-fired stove to heat damp sand, in order to reduce moisture so that the sand would flow freely from the locomotive sand domes. The bins were for storage of sand. In the lower picture, a former D&RGW employee stood in the middle of the Sargent wye, pointed his camera south, and took this view. It includes one end of the turntable — located within the wye — the east side of the water tank, and (on the opposite side of the mainline), two Rio Grande combination cars, No. 211 and No. 214, still carrying "Baggage-Railway Express Agency" lettering on their sides. Behind the two cars is a store building.

D. E. ROGERS PHOTO – SUNDANCE COLLECTION

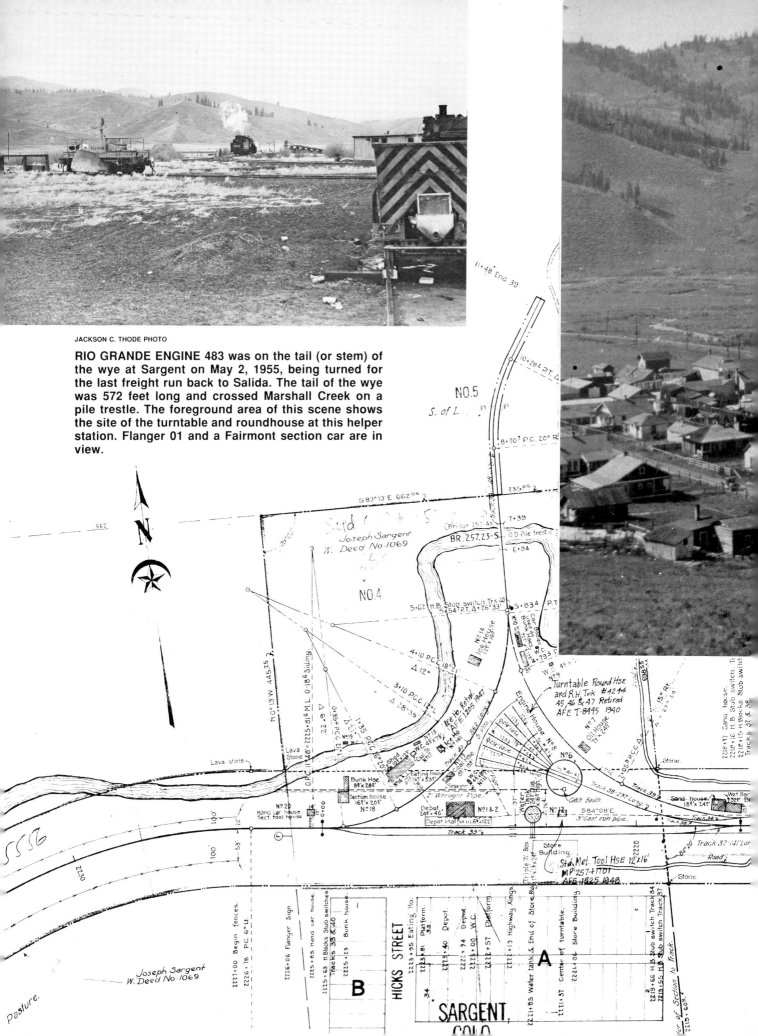

JACKSON C. THODE PHOTO

RIO GRANDE ENGINE 483 was on the tail (or stem) of the wye at Sargent on May 2, 1955, being turned for the last freight run back to Salida. The tail of the wye was 572 feet long and crossed Marshall Creek on a pile trestle. The foreground area of this scene shows the site of the turntable and roundhouse at this helper station. Flanger 01 and a Fairmont section car are in view.

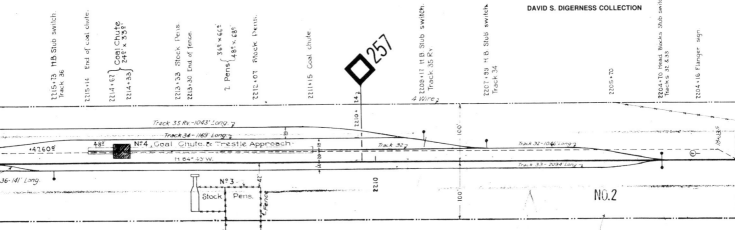

**D&RGW STATION MAP OF SARGENT
COURTESY OF JOHN W. MAXWELL
COLLECTION**

THE TOWN OF SARGENT appeared like this in 1926. The photographer was looking north, across the mainline at the depot, eating house (beyond the depot) and the six-stall roundhouse and turntable. Several coal cars (gondolas) had been spotted near the end-of-track on the tail of the wye. A large part of Sargent's population was made up of D&RGW employees.

A CONCENTRATION of Sargent depot views are illustrated on these two pages. A Rocky Mountain Railroad Club excursion train — with Engine 494 on the point — had arrived beside the water tank on September 18, 1948. At left, the rear wall of the depot looked like this after abandonment of the railroad. Below: An excellent view is reproduced here of the mainline side of the depot, with a bay window for the telegraph operator, as well as the station sign and train-order board (a hand-operated signal). The eating house stands at the left, across the west leg of the wye.

ABOVE (RIGHT), No. 483 was heading the the last westbound train over Marshall Pass on May 2, 1955. The engine had just arrived at the Sargent depot., with a long train of empty gondolas for the dismantler. Notice the SARGENT station sign on the front of the depot.

OPPOSITE: D&RG 2–8–0 No. 404 was standing on a track in the Sargent helper station just after returning from a helper assignment on Marshall Pass during the summer of 1907. Notice that the order board was in the stop position (red), and No. 404 was carrying rather grimy white "extra" flags, which had been used on her run back down the pass from the summit.

ED CRIST PHOTO – RICHARD A. RONZIO COLLECTION

DELL A. McCOY PHOTO

**ROYAL GORGE ROUTE**

**D & R G W R R**

**SCENIC LINE**

1926 – 1936

IN THIS VIEW you are looking west during 1955, and you can see that the turntable and roundhouse had been removed. The eating house, coalshed and outhouse are near the flanger on this page. The lower photograph on Page 126 shows the back wall of the eating house. Below, Engines 483 and 489 were standing at Sargent after the last trip over Marshall Pass from Salida. Flanger 01 (at left) was in the yard on May 2, 1955. At a later date, the Sargent depot was trucked to Gunnison for public display at the Gunnison Pioneer Museum, with locomotive No. 268 (a C-16 2–8–0), the water tank from Mears Junction and other pieces of rolling stock.

RICHARD H. KINDIG PHOTO

E. J. HALEY PHOTO

D&RGW LOCOMOTIVE NO. 483 was taking on water at the Sargent tank on May 2, 1955, in preparation for the return to Salida. This train was the last D&RGW freight train operated over Marshall Pass. Notice the Fairmont section car, which had been set off the mainline rails.

IN THE ABOVE VIEW (next page), No. 489 had pulled forward so that her tender tank could be filled for the same trip over the pass, May 2, 1955. The caboose, just behind No. 489, housed the train's conductor and the rear-end brakeman. The caboose on the tail end had been added to the consist for a group of fortunate railfans.

THE LOWER PICTURE was taken during the winter at Sargent, and it shows the effects of long stretches of cold weather at the water tank. In the distance, the mainline headed toward Marshall Pass — now covered by snow and ice. The sandhouse and coaling station are in view down the line, with a gondola spotted on the long siding.

1939 – 1948

129

ROBERT W. RICHARDSON PHOTO – COLORADO RAILROAD MUSEUM

AT THE WEST END of the Sargent yard, No. 489 was backing out of the wye to head east on the mainline in order to take on water for the trip over Marshall Pass, May 2, 1955. A small section house, with attached car body for bunking, can be seen at the right.

A FORMER RAILBUS from the Rio Grande Southern — a "Galloping Goose" — had been modified so it could be used by the dismantler while scrapping the D&RGW line over Marshall Pass. It was photographed while at Sargent on August 13, 1955. The front end of the railbus was originally a Pierce-Arrow limousine, an expensive automobile when it was produced during the late 1920's.

JACKSON C. THODE PHOTO

OTTO C. PERRY PHOTO – E. J. HALEY COLLECTION

Built N.G. to Gunnison in 1881, to Sapinero in 1882.

**THE PHOTOGRAPHER** found the fast-running passenger train, the "Shavano" — below Sargent — rolling along on her last run, November 24, 1940. The 2–8–2 K-28, No. 479, affectionately called "sports models" by employees and railfans alike, was hauling a Railway Express Agency / baggage car, as well as a Railway Post Office car (No. 80), a baggage car, coach and a parlor car (at the tail end). After the Shavano's passenger run was abandoned, many would say, "The mail service sure went bad after the passenger train quit running."

**THE DRUMHEAD** on the parlor car at the tail end of the "Shavano" passenger train was photographed while it was standing at Sargent.

ELMORE FREDERICK COLLECTION

| | 8288 | 8168 | 8062 | | 7952 | 7796 | | Jct Pt Crested Butte Br. 288.56 |
|---|---|---|---|---|---|---|---|---|
| | | Pump | | Sargent to Iola 8" Gr. Ballast put in | | Pump | | 7683 T.T. 60 ft. - Wye |
| | | | | | | | | Pump |
| 6° | 5° | 2° | 6° | | 4° | 4° | | |
| -1.28 | -1.00 | -0.90 | -0.50 | | -0.75 | -0.67 +0.34 | | |
| | | | | | | | | |
| 262.05 ELKO | 265.48 CROOKTON | 269.46 DOYLE | | 276.82 PARLIN | | 282.16 MOUNDS | | 288.64 GUNNISON (Ou Depot) |
| | | | | 65# | | | | |
| | | 1898 | | | | 1897 | | |
| 263.53 | | | 273.32 | | | 287.84 | | |

260          280

**THE RANCHERS** of the Gunnison Country often pooled their cattle shipments for a trainload out of the region. The 489 was photographed near Parlin on October 9, 1953, with this livestock train, as it headed for Sargent and the climb over Marshall Pass to Salida.

**D&RGW TRAIN NO. 315,** the westbound "Shavano," was being hauled by No. 499 on July 4, 1940, en route to Gunnison, with its usual consist. Tomichi Creek meanders through this long mountain meadow, which is irrigated by the stream, turning the valley into a verdant dale, in what is normally a fairly arid region — much of which is typical Colorado cattle-and-sheep country.

JOHN W. MAXWELL PHOTO

**THE TREELESS HILLSIDES** around Doyle — about 20 miles east of Gunnison —
are evident in this view of No. 483, as she set out a string of gondolas. The K-36
2–8–2 was backing through the turnout on June 26, 1951.

**ELKO** — Milepost 262.0, Elevation 8,288 feet —
had a siding capable of holding 45 cars (1,782 feet
long).

**CROOKTON** — Milepost 265.5, Elevation 8,168
feet — had a relative short siding capable of holding only 22 cars.

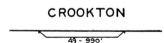

**DOYLE** — Milepost 269.5, Elevation 8,062 feet —
had a siding with a capacity of only 18 cars.

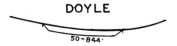

**BONITA** — Milepost 270.4 — had a siding capacity of 44 cars (1,745 feet long).

**PARLIN** — Milepost 276.8, Elevation 7,952 feet
— had a water tank and a siding with a capacity
for 29 cars. There was also a single-ended spur on
the north side of the passing siding. It was at this
point where the South Park line entered the
Tomichi Valley to parallel the D&RG for the
nearly 12 miles on into Gunnison.

**STEELE** (originally Cochetopa) — Milepost
282.2, Elevation 7,796 feet — had a siding with a
capacity for 41 cars (1,648 feet long).

133

EASTBOUND MIKADO NO. 489 had a trainload of scrap rail in tow when photographed at Parlin on May 24, 1955. The 489 was assigned to scrap-train duties over Marshall Pass. Parlin — in the Tomichi Valley east of Gunnison — was once served by both the South Park and Rio Grande railroads. However, the Colorado & Southern (ex-Denver, South Park & Pacific) gave up its Alpine Tunnel route to Gunnison in 1910, and the D&RGW's Marshall Pass line to Gunnison had sat idle from 1953 until scrapping took place some two years later. The D&RGW line over Marshall Pass was part of the original east-west narrow-gauge mainline between Denver and the Salt Lake area. After CF&I shut down its coal-mining industry in the Gunnison Country, the Rio Grande's Marshall Pass line became excess baggage.

# DENVER AND RIO GRANDE
## RAILROAD SYSTEM

*Parlins.*

1972' to M.P. 278

Land claimed by D.&R.G.

**D&RG STATION MAP – PARLINS – 1889**

Tomichi Creek

**IN THE SURROUNDING AREA** near Gunnison, the land was quite fertile, and many ranchers have done well in this hilly region. Eastbound locomotive No. 489 had a load of scrap rail from the Baldwin Branch on May 24, 1955.

**ON JUNE 5, 1941,** the photographer found No. 479 in Gunnison, with passenger cars tacked on behind. The yard had several gondolas loaded with coal at this time. No. 479 was performing switching duties when the photographer recorded this scene.

| READ DOWN | | Miles | STATIONS | Eleva-tion | READ UP | |
|---|---|---|---|---|---|---|
| | 15-315 | | | | 316-16 | |
| | * 7.30PM | 0.0 | Lv. . .DENVER. . .Ar | 5280 | * 7.45AM | |
| | 9.50PM | 74.9 | Lv Colorado Springs Ar | 5989 | 5.05AM | |
| | 11.25PM | 119.4 | Lv. . . PUEBLO. . . .Ar | 4668 | 3.45AM | |
| | 12.22AM | 151.9 | Lv. . FLORENCE . . Lv | 5199 | 2.33AM | |
| | 12.50AM | 160.0 | Lv. . .Canon City. . Ar | 5344 | 2.10AM | |
| | | 164.8 | . . . . .Royal Gorge. . . . . | 5494 | | |
| | ‡ 2.55AM | 215.1 | Ar. . . .SALIDA. . . .Lv | 7050 | 12.01AM | |
| | * 7.15AM | 215.1 | Lv. . . .SALIDA. . . .Ar | 7050 | * 11.00PM | |
| | f 7.50AM | 226.0 | Lv Mears Junction .Lv | 8431 | f 10.25PM | |
| | 8.50AM | 240.7 | Ar. .Marshall Pass. .Lv | 10856 | 9.30PM | |
| | 9.45AM | 257.2 | Lv. . .Sargent. . . .Ar | 8477 | 8.33PM | |
| | 10.12AM | 269.5 | Ar. . .Doyle. . . .Lv | 8062 | 8.05PM | |
| | 10.28AM | 276.8 | Ar. . .Parlin. . . .Lv | 7952 | 7.50PM | |
| | ‡ 10.55AM | 288.6 | Ar. .Gunnison. . .Lv | 7683 | 7.25PM | |
| Rio Grande Motor Way, Inc. | ¶ 11.15AM | 288.6 | Lv. . GUNNISON . .Ar | 7683 | ¶ 6.30PM | Rio Grande Motor Way, Inc. |
| | ¶ 11.50AM | 299.4 | Lv. . .Almont. . .Lv | 8042 | ¶ 5.51PM | |
| | ¶ 12.10PM | 304.7 | Lv. .Jacks Cabin. .Lv | 8309 | ¶ 5.33PM | |
| | ¶ 12.50PM | 316.3 | Ar. .Crested Butte. .Lv | 8878 | ¶ 5.00PM | |
| | | 288.6 | Lv. . GUNNISON . .Ar | 7683 | | |
| | | 276.8 | Lv. . .Parlin. . .Lv | 7952 | | |
| | | 285.2 | Ar. . .Ohio City. . .Lv | | | |
| | | 291.9 | Ar. . .PITKIN. . . .Lv | 9188 | | |
| | | 288.6 | Lv. . GUNNISON . .Ar | 7683 | | |
| | | 305.8 | Ar. . .BALDWIN. . .Lv | | | |
| | * 11.15AM | 288.6 | Lv. . . .Gunnison. . .Ar | 7683 | ‡ 7.05PM | |
| | f 11.40AM | 299.2 | Ar. . . .Iola. . . .Lv | 7450 | ‡ 6.40PM | |
| | f 12.01PM | 307.1 | Ar. . .Cebolla. . .Lv | 7354 | f 6.20PM | |
| | 12.20PM | 314.0 | Ar. . .Sapinero. . .Lv | 7255 | * 6.01PM | |
| | | 314.0 | Lv. . .SAPINERO. . .Ar | 7255 | | |
| | | 328.0 | Ar. . .Madera. . .Lv | | | |
| | | 350.5 | Ar. .LAKE CITY. .Lv | 8686 | | |
| Service Discontinued | | 329.0 | Ar. .Cimarron. . .Lv | 6905 | 5.13PM | Service Discontinued |
| | * 1.11PM | 351.5 | Ar. .MONTROSE. .Lv | 5811 | * 3.35PM | |
| | 2.40PM | | | | | |
| Mixed | † 4.15PM | 351.5 | Lv. . .MONTROSE. .Ar | 5811 | † 1.30PM | Mixed |
| | 5.57PM | 377.1 | Lv. . .Ridgway. . .Ar | 7003 | 12.01PM | |
| | 6.45PM | 387.4 | Ar. . .OURAY. . .Lv | 7721 | 11.15AM | |
| | | | (R. G. S. R. R.) | | | |
| | * 6.10PM | 377.1 | Lv. . .RIDGWAY . .Ar | 7003 | * 11.45AM | |
| | 9.10PM | 422.2 | Ar. .TELLURIDE. .Lv | 8756 | 8.45AM | |
| | * 7.00AM | 422.2 | Lv. .TELLURIDE. .Ar | 8756 | * 4.00PM | |
| | 9.05AM | 443.3 | Ar. . . .Rico. . . . .Lv | 8737 | 1.55PM | |
| | 11.00AM | 479.4 | Ar. . .Dolores. . . .Lv | 6957 | 12.01PM | |
| | 1.13PM | 499.6 | Ar. . .Mancos. . .Lv | 7008 | 10.05AM | |
| | 3.20PM | 539.2 | Ar. .DURANGO. .Lv | 6520 | 8.00AM | |
| | * 3.45PM | 351.5 | Lv. . .MONTROSE. .Ar | 5811 | * 3.15PM | |
| | 4.07PM | 362.2 | Lv. . .Olathe. . . .Lv | 5365 | 2.52PM | |
| | 4.33PM | 372.8 | Ar. . . .DELTA. . . .Lv | 4980 | 2.30PM | |
| Rio Grande Motor Way, Inc. | ¶ 4.40PM | 372.8 | Lv. . . .DELTA. . . .Ar | 4980 | ¶ 10.15AM | Rio Grande Motor Way, Inc. |
| | ¶ 5.00PM | 380.8 | Lv. . . .Austin. . . .Lv | 5070 | ¶ 9.30AM | |
| | | 393.2 | Lv. . . .Lazear. . . .Lv | 5443 | | |
| | ¶ 5.45PM | 397.8 | Lv. .HOTCHKISS. .Lv | 5369 | ¶ 8.45AM | |
| | ¶ 6.20PM | 405.9 | Ar. . .PAONIA. . .Lv | 5694 | ¶ 8.00AM | |
| | ¶ 7.40PM | 415.3 | Ar. .SOMERSET. .Lv | 6065 | ¶ 7.00AM | |
| | * 4.33PM | 372.8 | Lv. . . .DELTA. . . .Ar | 4980 | 2.30PM | |
| | f 5.51PM | 411.8 | Ar. . .Whitewater. .Lv | 4665 | f 1.15PM | |
| | 6.25PM | 424.2 | Ar. GRAND JUNCTION Lv | 4583 | * 12.45PM | |

**D&RGW LOCOMOTIVE NO. 347** had just arrived at the Gunnison station on its run from Salida, c. 1939. With her fluted domes and old box headlight (now electrified), the Class C-19 2–8–0 Consolidation looks much as it did prior to her renumbering in 1924, when the engine lost its number "407."

**GUNNISON** — Milepost 288.4, Elevation 7,683 feet — was reached on August 6, 1881, and the first passenger train steamed into town on Monday, August 8, 1881, powered by D&RG engine No. 46, the *Badito* — a Class 56 2–8–0. This Consolidation had been built by the Baldwin Locomotive Works the previous year, so she was relatively new.

A large single-story wooden depot (24 feet x 155 feet, similar to the one at Silverton) — painted buff, with dark-brown trim — had been built beside the mainline. The depot was inside a wye, where the Crested Butte Branch left the mainline (at Milepost 288.55).

West of the Gunnison depot and wye, the D&RG had put up a wooden freight house (24 feet x 200 feet) and a two-stall car-repair shed. Just south of the car-repair shop was a stone-and-brick 11-stall roundhouse, served by an 80-foot turntable. Gunnison's standard wooden water tank and pumphouse were located near the beginning of the main roundhouse lead track, while the coaling tower and sandhouse were next in line with the buff-and-brown water tank — a wooden structure virtually identical with the coaling tipple still standing in the former Rio Grande terminal at Chama, New Mexico. An ashpit was located on the lead track, adjacent to the turntable.

JOSEPH SCHICK PHOTO – ELMORE FREDERICK COLLECTION

**THE ROCKY MOUNTAIN RAILROAD CLUB** chartered a special passenger run through the Black Cañon of the Gunnison, photographed here at the Gunnison passenger depot on September 19, 1948. Members and guests stand alongside the train as they wait for its westbound departure from the Gunnison depot — seen in the background.

**THE D&RGW'S "SILVER VISTA,"** the railroad's home-built glass-topped observation car, was on the rear of this Rio Grande excursion train (below). Although it had rained most of the previous night, September 19, 1948, turned out to be a beautiful day. This brick depot had been erected on the site of the old Gunnison Sampler, shown on the next page. Depot accommodations had previously been available at the spacious La Veta Hotel.

RICHARD H. KINDIG PHOTO

**GUNNISON'S LA VETA HOTEL** still had her grand and very pleasing Victorian appearance during the pre-war year of 1940. And except for the rather tasteless sign placed atop the roof, the "old lady" was still a wonder from a glorious era of long, long ago. Ornamental ironwork was missing from the roof, but the old building was still worth saving — something too many of the residents of Gunnison failed to appreciate. At any rate, the beautiful old hotel was demolished after World War II with hardly so much as a whimper of protest — with only the ground floor remaining today. A glimpse of the D&RGW track can be seen crossing the street at this location. Gondolas stand on this track, once used by the railroad's passenger trains.

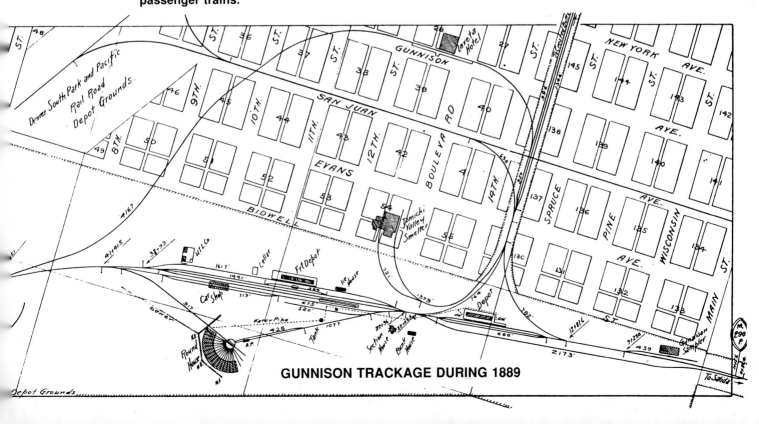

**GUNNISON TRACKAGE DURING 1889**

THE D&RGW ROUNDHOUSE at Gunnison saw a lot of railroad men come and go through the years. Some of them had deep feelings for the place, and they erected a memorial to the earlier years of the Denver & Rio Grande. A flagpole in the center of a circle of white rocks had an entrance pathway with link-and-pin drawheads on either side. This picture was shot on September 11, 1940, not long before the U.S. became involved in World War II. The little narrow-gauge line was an important transportation link during the war years, and Rio Grande men took pride in the fact. D&RGW Engine 472 occupied space on the turntable, while No. 454 was on the west lead track. A drop-bottom gondola had been filled with locomotive ashes, shoveled from the ashpit, where engine grates were cleaned. To the right stands the sandhouse and sand-storage bin.

JACKSON C. THODE COLLECTION

DAVID S. DIGERNESS COLLECTION

LOOKING DOWN THE EAST LEAD track toward the depot, the water tank and coaling station are beyond the two road engines that had just arrived for servic-ing. On the next page (below), No. 489 was ready to take on water before hauling scrap rail to Poncha Junction on May 24, 1955 — part of the dismantling opera-tions of the scrapper. The car-repair shop is at far right.

140

RICHARD H. KINDIG PHOTO

D&RG ENGINE NO. 173 was built by Baldwin Locomotive Works in 1884. The 4–6–0 driver arrangement and tractive effort classified the locomotive as a T-12, and she was called a Ten-wheeler — best suited for comparitively fast-running with light passenger trains. Unfortunately, No. 173 was scrapped in 1926.

HERE WE SEE a work train in the Gunnison yard during August of 1935. It consisted of narrow-gauge D&RGW locomotive No. 201, a "drag" flanger and an outfit car (among others). No. 201 was a C-16 built by the Grant works in 1881.

THE THREE LOCOMOTIVES on the next page illustrate more of the motive power that was available in Gunnison. At the top, the little No. 223 — built by Grant Locomotive Works in 1881 — was photographed in 1940. The Baldwin-built No. 278 of 1882 vintage is shown twice on this page — for views of both left and right sides of the engine — as the C-16 rested in the Gunnison yard. Notice the old-time flanged (or "fluted") domes on this Consolidation.

D. E. ROGERS PHOTO – SUNDANCE COLLECTION

THE THREE PHOTOGRAPHS on the preceeding page show three more freight locomotives built by Baldwin. No. 317 was a bit smaller than the 340-series 2–8–0's on these two pages. No. 317 was classified as a C-18 and had come from the Florence & Cripple Creek in 1917 (the famous "Gold Belt" narrow-gauge line). Originally, the engine was a Class 72 2–8–0, built for the F&CC as their No. 5 by Baldwin in 1895, and named the "Florence." She was being backed onto the Gunnison turntable. No. 340 was photographed on June 1, 1939, and the 341 was photographed on September 20, 1936.

NUMBERS 344 AND 345 — C-19 2–8–0's — were assigned to haul freight and passenger trains through the Black Cañon of the Gunnison, west of the town of Gunnison. This was mainly because the rail and bridge construction had not been designed for anything larger than C-21 Class engines.

D. E. ROGERS PHOTO – SUNDANCE COLLECTION

RAY W. BUHRMASTER PHOTO – DAVID S. DIGERNESS COLLECTION

THE EX-CRYSTAL RIVER locomotives, constructed by Baldwin in 1900, were unusual for their time, built with outside frames because of their larger size. No. 360 was photographed on September 18, 1948, in Gunnison. A former Crystal River Railroad locomotive, outside-frame 2–8–0 No. 102, was sold to the D&RGW in 1916, and she was renumbered "361," and eventually was classified as a C-21 (in 1923) — along with sister engine, No. 360 (ex-CRR No. 101). This train was headed west, and a glimpse of the Gunnison depot is in view (at left).

OPPOSITE: The photographer found C-21 No. 361 on the Gunnison turntable. No. 463, a K-27, had just arrived in Gunnison for road service during 1903. She was equipped with a slope-back tender, suitable for a switcher, but not so good for a road engine. And the 2–8–2 had unusual cylinders and valve gear, due to having been constructed by Baldwin as four-cylinder Vauclain compounds. They were subsequently converted, with "D" slide valves (between 1907 and 1909). The 474 was yet another size larger in the D&RGW's narrow-gauge engine designs. Larger airpumps had been placed ahead of the smoke box on this K-28 Class of "Mikes." The K-28's were specifically designed to haul passenger trains, and they were commonly called "sports models."

RAY W. BUHRMASTER PHOTO – DAVID S. DIGERNESS COLLECTION

**A LARGER LOCOMOTIVE** was put into service in 1925, and was designated as the K-36 Class 2–8–2. This was the last order placed with Baldwin by the D&RGW for narrow-gauge engines. These husky machines were the main locomotives used between Gunnison and Salida via Marshall Pass.

**THE LAST-NUMBERED** narrow-gauge locomotive on the D&RGW — No. 499 — was used for a Rocky Mountain Railroad Club excursion. This view was photographed on September 7, 1947, after the train had come over Marshall Pass into Gunnison.

JOHN W. MAXWELL PHOTO

D&RGW K-37 NO. 498 was on the turntable at the Gunnison roundhouse on June 2, 1947, after being called-up for a work train that will run to Crested Butte. The 490-series locomotives were constructed by the D&RGW in their Burnham shops in Denver during 1928. Their boilers were from standard-gauge 2–8–0's of the C-41 Class. They were built as outside-frame 2–8–2's, the largest narrow-gauge locomotives to run on the D&RGW system. The engineer's side of the 498 appears below — photographed on the same date.

JOHN W. MAXWELL PHOTO

D. E. ROGERS PHOTO – SUNDANCE COLLECTION

**A MOUNTAIN RAILROAD** needed a lot of back-up equipment on hand to keep the system open during winter months, as snowstorms dumped many feet of powder snow on the right-of-way — sometimes nearly every day. This old wedge plow was photographed in Gunnison on August 11, 1935. A headlight was mounted up high for night-time snowplowing. In 1903, rotary snowplow No. 2 appeared to be in good condition, ready to be called into service whenever required.

HORACE CURTISS PHOTO – E. J. HALEY COLLECTION

ROBERT W. RICHARDSON PHOTO – WILLIAM R. JONES COLLECTION

**THE FORMER CRYSTAL RIVER** rotary snowplow, No. AB2, was purchased by the D&RGW in 1916 and redesignated as the "OO." The machine was photographed in Gunnison. The two detailed views of the rotary (lower left) were made in the Gunnison roundhouse during August of 1953. The arrangement of the doors and windows on the operator's side of No. OO can be seen in the picture below, taken near the coaling station in Gunnison.

JACK MORISON PHOTO

ROBERT SHANK SR. PHOTO

ROBERT SHANK SR. PHOTO

ROBERT W. RICHARDSON PHOTO – WILLIAM R. JONES COLLECTION

**NO. 486 WAS CLEANING SNOW** out of the Gunnison yard with a flanger after one of the many winter storms in the area. Caboose 0524 (below) had been spotted beside the car-repair shed in Gunnison. This was one of the short cabooses used by the D&RGW.

WILLIAM H. RADCLIFFE PHOTO – DAVID S. DIGERNESS COLLECTION

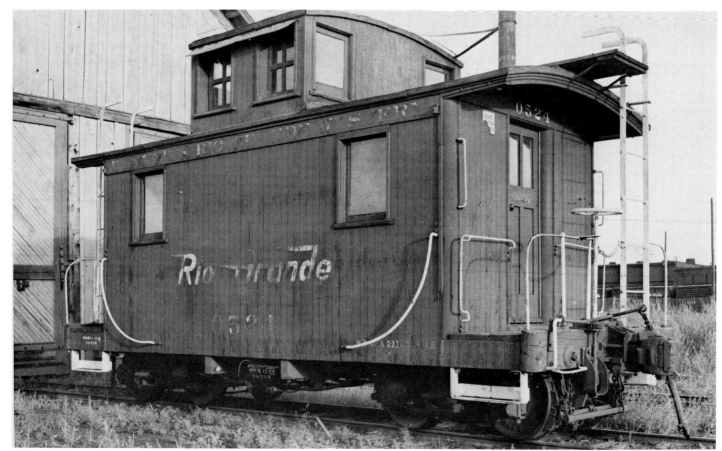

NEAL MILLER PHOTO

ON MAY 30, 1949, Numbers 495 and 491 were ready for departure at Gunnison, with an eastbound freight train, hauling Crested Butte coal over Marshall Pass to Salida. The engines will doublehead to the helper station of Sargent, take on coal and water, and then the 495 will be cut into the consist for the climb up the 4.0-percent grade to the pass. At the left is the "Silver Vista" open-air observation car, tacked onto the Rocky Mountain Railroad Club's last trip through the scenic Black Cañon of the Gunnison.

THE LITTLE NO. 278 — below and on the next two pages — was assigned to work livestock movements on the Crested Butte Branch out of Gunnison, shown here during August of 1951. It is amazing how two small C-16's could move so much tonnage — illustrated overleaf, backing a train near Gunnison, with a long caboose bringing up the rear.

PHILIPP A. RONFOR PHOTO – E. J. HALEY COLLECTION

**THE 268 WAS ALL BUT DEAD** — with only a wisp of steam emerging from the blow-off valve after her fire had been dropped and the boiler had been drained.

**JUST BEFORE SUNSET** on June 30, 1955, No. 268 brought her last trainload of scrap rail into Gunnison. The car-repair shed is in the background of this scene.

RICHARD H. KINDIG PHOTO

ENGINE 268 WAS PUSHING the dismantling train past the former Denver, South
Park & Pacific depot in Gunnison, as it was on the way to help tear up track on
the Baldwin Branch near Castleton, on May 24, 1955.

# THE LAST RUN OF D&RGW ENGINE NO. 268
## — A Narrow-Gauge Vignette —
### By Robert A. LeMassena

COMMENCING IN 1949, with the removal of
track between Sapinero and Cedar Creek, the Denver & Rio Grande Western Railroad started to dis-
mantle its narrow-gauge lines west of Salida. This
was followed by the segment between Mears Junction and Hooper in 1951, and between Montrose–Cedar Creek and Ridgway–Ouray in 1953.
During 1955, the Baldwin and Crested Butte
branches, as well as the mainline between Sapinero
and Poncha Junction, were dismantled. Thus, Gunnison, which had been the busy hub of railroad activity in the Gunnison River Valley, found itself
without railroad service. There were reasons enough
for what the D&RGW had done. The coal mines at
Baldwin and Kubler had ceased production; cattle
and sheep were being moved by motor trucks on
improved highways; and the Rio Grande Southern
had quit operating in 1951.

During better years, the D&RGW brought four
engines to Gunnison to move trains over the light
rail and under-maintained roadbed of the branches.
Two ex-Crystal River outside-frame 2–8–0's, numbered 360 and 361, worked between Gunnison and

Cerro Summit. They remained active through 1951.
The two others, numbered 268 and 278, were me-
chanical antiquities, having been constructed by the
Baldwin works in 1882. Almost overnight, these
two 2–8–0's became the two oldest operating locomotives on the railroad, and the only ones of their
type — Class C-16 (formerly Class 60) Consolida-
tions. The 278 was retired in 1953, leaving the 268
as the sole survivor.

In early October of 1953, No. 268 pulled the
last stock train from Iola to Gunnison. A year later,
on October 5, 1954, this little 2–8–0 hauled the last
train between Sapinero and Gunnison, clearing all
the remaining cars from the line — and then com-
menced hauling the dismantling train. No. 268 went
to work again the following May, when the Baldwin Branch and the Gunnison yard trackage were
removed. In June, the engine worked with the scrap
train on the Crested Butte Branch, but was replaced
by a K-36 2–8–2, No. 489, on July 1, 1955. Thus,
its last trip from Jacks Cabin into Gunnison was a
grand finalé to the Denver & Rio Grande Western's
long-lived narrow-gauge 2–8–0's.

157

**ON OCTOBER 10, 1953, No. 268** — painted in "bumblebee" livery — dumped her ashes at Gunnison. Below, out on the line, No. 268 was equipped to take on river water while working with the dismantling crew.

JOHN KRAUSE PHOTO – DAVID S. DIGERNESS COLLECTION

**IT WAS JUNE OF 1952,** and the 268 was busy moving a freight train downriver out of Gunnison toward Sapinero.

**IN 1948, C-16 NO. 268** was placed on display in Denver's Civic Center, along with a U.S. Air Force missile. The 2–8–0 had been painted in garish Rio Grande gold and black for an appearance at the Chicago Railroad Fair of 1948.

DELL A. McCOY PHOTO

After leaving its train, the 268 proceded to the water tank, where its fire was dropped, and the boiler was drained of its remaining water. As the roar of steam from the blow-off valve subsided to a barely audible hiss, those who witnessed this event realized that it was actually the end of an era, which had begun with the delivery of the railroad's first 2–8–0 in 1877.

Fortunately, both the 278 and the 268 have been preserved; the 278 rests on a bridge near Cimarron, and the 268 is in a park at Gunnison. No. 278 is very dramatically displayed, along with a 3,000-series boxcar and a short caboose on a high bridge over the Cimarron River — just upstream from its confluence with the Gunnison River in the Black Cañon. Both approaches to the bridge have been removed so that vandals cannot reach the little train. No. 268 is prominently on display in Gunnison.

DELL A. McCOY PHOTO

# ADVENTURE TRAILS OF NORTHERN GUNNISON COUNTY

## By Ron Ruhoff

*A*S THE *Trails Among the Columbine* series continues, northern Gunnison County, in the vicinity of Crested Butte, will be the focal point. The high jagged ridges of the Elk Mountain Range, which form the divide between the drainages of the Gunnison River to the south and the Crystal and Roaring Fork rivers to the north, will be explored.

The many high passes, accessible by four-wheel-drive vehicle, mountain bike or on foot, are numerous in this area. And it is the object of this story to cover each one, with visits to many side canyons along the way. Ghost towns, railroad and mining history, and some of the grandest vistas in Colorado await those who wish to explore the high country of this region.

I would strongly suggest having copies of the Gunnison National Forest and White River Na-

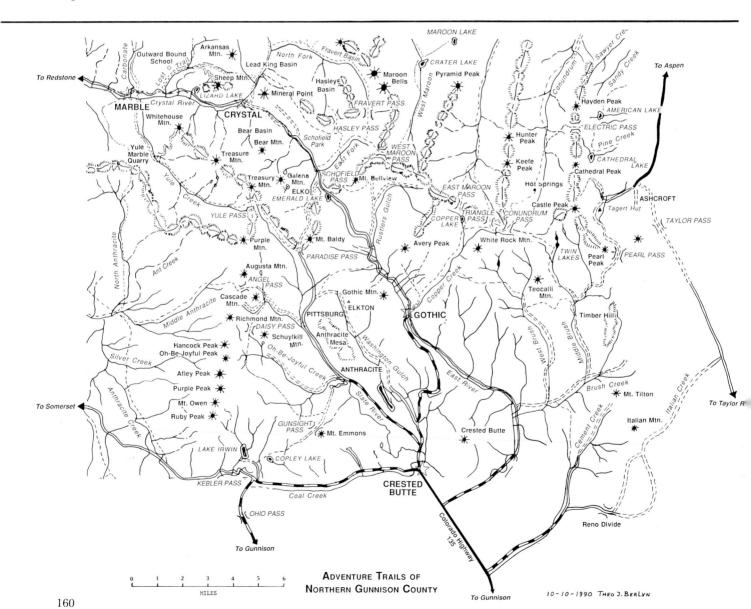

ADVENTURE TRAILS OF
NORTHERN GUNNISON COUNTY

10-10-1990 THEO J. BERLYN

tional Forest maps, as well as the more detailed U.S. Geological Survey (USGS) quad maps for trail and road information. The map included herein covers the major features of the land.

Upon arriving in the town of Crested Butte, a panorama of the Elk Mountains begins to unfold. The most prominant mountain, of course, is 12,162-foot Crested Butte itself. This peak, as well as the nearby Gothic Mountain, were first called "The Crested Buttes" by Ferdinand V. Hayden, while he headed the U.S. government surveys in the 1870's. The name stuck on the most visible mountain, and the adjacent mining town took on the name as well. Mount Whetstone rises directly south of the town to a height of 12,543 feet, and the Gibson Ridge and 12,055-foot Mount Axtell can be seen to the southwest. The large Jokerville coal mine, opened by the Colorado Coal & Iron Company (now CF&I Steel Corporation) in 1881, was located beneath the Gibson Ridge, which was named for pit boss John Gibson.

The Jokerville mine was noted for its dangerous pockets of explosive gas, which led to the disastrous explosion in 1884, which killed 59 miners. A visit to the Crested Butte cemetery today is suggested to witness the mass grave of these miners, which carries upon a single stone the epitaph:

> *Their lives were gentle*
> *And the elements so mixed in them,*
> *that nature might stand up and*
> *say to all the world:*
> *"They were men."*

**THE COLOR VIEW ABOVE was recorded during July of 1989. It shows the graves of the 59 miners who lost their lives in the Jokerville mine disaster of 1884. These historic gravestones can be visited today in the Crested Butte Cemetery.**

Ironically, a similar disaster occurred in Crested Butte on March 6, 1990, when an explosion demolished the Crested Butte State Bank building, killing three people. Although still under investigation (as of this writing), it is believed to have been caused by seepage of propane gas from nearby pipelines. This prompted the construction of a new natural-gas pipeline from Gunnison, which was installed along the highway right-of-way during the summer of 1990, in order to more safely serve the heating needs of the community.

**THIS SCENE was photographed in 1984 and shows the Crested Butte State Bank before the gas explosion of March 6, 1990. The building was totally destroyed, and three employees were killed in the mysterious blast.**

Northwest of Crested Butte lies 12,392-foot Mount Emmons, which shows on its south face obvious evidence of mining activity. The Keystone mine, located within the mountain, was an original silver producer, which died with the infamous Silver Panic of 1893. In the 1950's, The American Smelting & Refining Company reopened the Keystone mine, built a large processing mill and produced large quantities of lead, zinc, copper and silver through the 1960's. During more recent years, AMAX, Inc. came close to developing a molybdenum mine on Mount Emmons, which sparked a good deal of local opposition. The people of Crested Butte simply did not want another Climax mine in their backyards. As it turned out, molybdenum lost its market value, and the Climax mine near Leadville was closed, while the Henderson mine, near Empire, Colorado — also owned by AMAX — cut its production drastically.

**IN THIS PHOTOGRAPH you are looking west along Crested Butte's Elk Avenue in 1950, while the matching black-and-white view (below) was taken during the early days of this colorful mining town. At least one false-fronted building can be seen in both views — on the right.**

RON RUHOFF PHOTO

**THE CRESTED BUTTE City Hall is portrayed here as it appeared during September of 1959. This beautiful building has survived since 1883, even though it suffered considerable damage on January 9, 1893, when an explosion tore a gaping hole in its east side during a major fire in the town. The structure remains today on Elk Avenue. The view below shows how City Hall looked after the explosion and fire of 1893.**

MERLE AND AUDREY DORSETT COLLECTION

Mount Emmons, as it happens, will be the first goal, as we begin our adventure trails into northern Gunnison County.

As the Coal Creek area was explored in last year's anthology, we will begin by following the Slate River toward its source. The name itself has been given to the river from the geology of the area through which it flows. The second-largest coal mine in the area — the Smith Hill — was located four miles above Crested Butte, where Oh-Be-Joyful Creek meets the Slate. Established in 1882, the Smith Hill mine produced high-grade anthracite coal and was served by a spur of the Denver & Rio Grande Western Railroad's narrow-gauge Crested Butte Branch until 1955. A community by the name of Anthracite built up around the mine, and at one time had close to 200 residents and its own post office and school. The grade of the large mine

163

**THE TOWN** of Crested Butte appears as shown above in 1959. The historic mining camp's namesake, prominent Crested Butte, rises high above the townsite.

**BELOW:** A group of climbers were enjoying a beautiful clear day atop the craggy 12,162-foot summit of Crested Butte during the summer of 1952.

THIS TELEPHOTO VIEW of the town of Crested Butte was shot from the summit of 12,162-foot Crested Butte. This viewpoint gives a map-like layout of the town — and the Coal Creek road to Kebler Pass may be easily seen in the background.

WHETSTONE MOUNTAIN, with a spring-time frosting of snow, rises above the Slate River Valley, just south of Crested Butte. This view (below) was made from the Skyland Camp during 1957 — present site of the Skyland Golf Course.

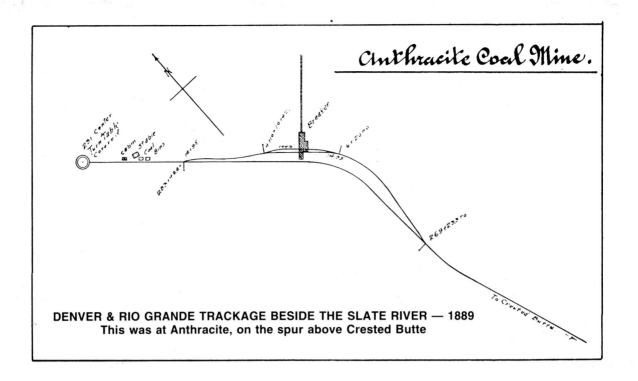

*Anthracite Coal Mine.*

**DENVER & RIO GRANDE TRACKAGE BESIDE THE SLATE RIVER — 1889**
This was at Anthracite, on the spur above Crested Butte

**THE VIEW BELOW** of 12,392-foot Mount Emmons was reflected in Grant Lake after a spring-time snowstorm. Skyland Camp was operated by Merle and Audrey Dorsett from 1949 until 1978, and it is the present-day site of the Skyland Golf Course. The town of Crested Butte can be seen at the far left.

RICHARD DAIS PHOTO

**FROM THE SMITH HILL** coal-mine site, high atop Anthracite Mesa, a fine view can be obtained of the Oh-Be-Joyful Gulch to the west. Smith Hill is accessible today from the Slate River road by turning right one and one-half miles above the junction of the highway to the ski resort of Mount Crested Butte.

**BELOW:** Writer/Editor Russ Collman was standing beside debris in this 1965 view of the site of the coal breaker at Smith Hill. This was on the grade of the D&RGW's spur to Anthracite (part of the Crested Butte Branch).

DELL A. McCOY PHOTO

RON RUHOFF PHOTOS

THE VIEW NORTHEAST from the top of 12,090-foot Gunsight Pass includes (from left to right): Snowmass Mountain, 14,093 feet; Hagerman Peak, 13,841 feet; Mount Bellview, 12,519 feet, with its striking reddish slopes; the Maroon Bells, 14,014 feet and 14,156 feet; Pyramid Peak, 14,018 feet; and Gothic Mountain, 12,625 feet.

WELL ABOVE TIMBERLINE on the approach to 12,090-foot Gunsight Pass, the final switchback to the top can be seen ahead on the north slope of Mount Emmons. The road to the summit of the pass is an excellent four-wheel-drive route today, but the back side to the Kebler Pass area is no longer driveable.

WHILE FOUR-WHEELING toward Gunsight Pass during 1990, this panoramic view was recorded. This scene was shot from the north side of Mount Emmons, near Crested Butte. From the remaining structures of the old Daisy mine, one can look ahead to the many hairline switchbacks of the road and the actual notch of Gunsight Pass, high above.

tramway, which led to the coal-breaker in the valley, may still be seen today. Coal slack still lies in large quantities around the road today. Several photographs of the Smith Hill operation were printed in the 1989 *Trails Among the Columbine*.

Directly across from the Smith Hill site is a sign marking the road to Gunsight Pass. For those who enjoy the thrill of a high mountain four-wheel-drive pass, Gunsight will be a must to explore. The road is in excellent shape today to the top of the pass; however, one cannot go on over to Elk Creek and Kebler Pass due to washouts on the west side. A short distance above the Slate River, it is necessary to go through a closed gate, which is no problem — just be sure to close it behind you. Many switchbacks will be negotiated as the road rises above timberline into Redwell Basin. Large ore-loading structures are still found on the left side of the road at the site of the Daisy mine, and at this location, views of the distant Elk Mountains begin to open up.

Ahead, the road is seen as a hairline of switchbacks cut through the talus slopes to the top of the pass. I always find it a thrill to drive such a road for the first time, as I look ahead with the anticipation of reaching the summit. The pass itself is suitably named, as the the road cuts through a high ridge in a narrow notch, which indeed looks just like a "gunsight." The views are fantastic in all directions.

To the northeast, all of the 14,000-foot peaks of the Elk Mountains are plainly visible. From left to right they are: Capitol Peak, 14,130 feet; Snowmass Mountain, 14,092 feet; the Maroon Bells, 14,014 feet and 14,150 feet; Pyramid Peak, 14,018 feet; and Castle Peak, 14,265 feet — as well as numerous other colorful peaks — are seen. Gothic Mountain stands out in the foreground to the northeast, and to its left, the mountain with the strikingly beautiful reddish west slope is 12,519-foot Mount Bellview, above Schofield Pass. To the southwest, near Floresta, the Anthracite Mountain Range is in the foreground. Then the West Elk Mountains and even the distant San Juan Mountains may be seen. On a clear day, Uncompahgre Peak — at an elevation of 14,309 feet — is easily recognizable.

Gunsight Pass is situated near the top of Mount Emmons, and the road continues around to the south side of the mountain (through a locked gate) to the mining properties. The pass road itself continues on down the west side into Evans Basin, but it is washed-out about a mile down the grade. One can drive on down to the washout, as I did in the summer of 1990, but I do not recommend it, unless you are adept at backing out. There is no room to turn around, and the road is rough and narrow.

Back to the Slate River road again, and just a

**A BEAUTIFUL WATERFALL** marks the entrance to Poverty Gulch, just above the location of the Pittsburg townsite. High in the distant alpine basin lies the site of the large Augusta gold-and-silver mine. One can drive to within about a mile of the mine today with a four-wheel-drive vehicle. Poverty Gulch offers an abundance of wildflowers and sparkling waterfalls.

half-mile above the junction of the Gunsight road, we will follow the Oh-Be-Joyful road. This four-wheel-drive road is another beauty to behold. It leads up into a high basin filled with wildflowers and waterfalls, as it follows Oh-Be-Joyful Creek into Democrat Basin. Much beautiful country surrounds this area, and it is accesible to the hiker and backpacker. Just south of Oh-Be-Joyful Gulch is

the Peeler Basin area, with many alpine lakes. The Daisy Pass trail traverses the area and is most easily followed from either the Daisy mine on the Gunsight road, or from the Poverty Gulch road through Baxter Basin. A copy of the Oh-Be-Joyful 7½-minute USGS quad map is suggested for this area.

Continuing north on the Slate River road, the ghost town of Pittsburg is located at the junction of Poverty Gulch. Today, Pittsburg is a true ghost town, in the sense that nothing at all remains to see at the site. It is on private property as well, and a number of summer homes exist in the area. Due to its proximity with large coal deposits, the settlement itself was named after the great Pennsylvania city of Pittsburgh (although the Colorado mining camp was incorrectly spelled "Pittsburg"). However, it was primarily a hard-rock mining camp, associated with the Augusta silver mine, high up in Poverty Gulch. The Augusta, Black Queen, Excelsior and Richmond mines produced silver ore in this area prior to the 1893 crash. The Pittsburg post office closed in 1896, and the town began its slide to ghost-town status.

Today's four-wheel-drive roads into Poverty Gulch offer scenery equal to the more famous Yankee Boy Basin, near Ouray in the San Juans. The waterfalls and wildflowers of Poverty Gulch are unsurpassed anywhere. About a mile and a half up the gulch, the road splits. The right-hand fork goes to the Augusta mine, but it is washed out at its crossing of the creek, near one of the large waterfalls.

A worthwhile hike to the Augusta mine site may be made from this point. The left-hand fork of the road offers easy four-wheeling high into Baxter Basin, and it ends at an old mine. Along the way, the road intersects with the Daisy Pass trail, and it is plainly marked with a Forest Service sign. On the way either up or down, it would be worthwhile to hike south of the roadway into the deep gulches of Baxter Creek for better viewpoints of the many spectacular and photogenic waterfalls not quite visible from the road.

From the Pittsburg townsite, the Slate River road continues to the north, and it is drivable with a regular automobile as far as Paradise Divide. Along the way, spectacular views of the Slate River Valley can be seen, as the road winds high above river level. In the distance, at the head of the Slate River Canyon, the old Yule Pass trail is plainly visible, cut into the talus slopes of Cinnamon Mountain — but more on that later.

RON RUHOFF PHOTOS

**THE TWO VIEWS on this page are of the beautiful Poverty Gulch waterfalls, located near the ghost town of Pittsburg.**

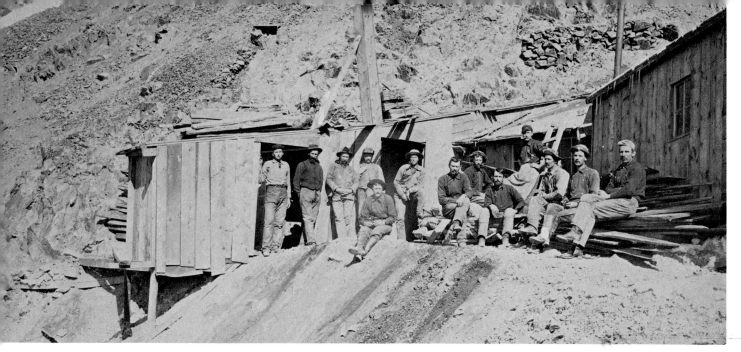

**THE AUGUSTA MINE in Poverty Gulch employed a rather large force of men in their search for valuable minerals. This was the day shift, and they were not at all reluctant to pose for this group photograph.**

**THE GHOST TOWN of Elkton, in Washington Gulch, looked like this during July of 1990. The townsite is privately owned, and it is lived-in today. It is accessed by a good road from Crested Butte, which connects through to the Paradise Pass road, above the old Painter Boy mine.**

Just beyond the long switchback of the road, a right-hand fork leads back into Washington Gulch, and this route offers a good road back to Crested Butte via the ghost town of Elkton. Even the Forest Service map does not indicate this as a drivable road, but it is open today. Four-wheel-drive vehicles will have no trouble between the road junction and Elkton, but I would caution against trying it in a car that is too long and low. Elkton itself is privately owned, but it offers several buildings to photograph today. You will pass the remains of the Painter Boy mine on the way to the townsite, which was a moderate silver producer in its day.

**THIS IS THE VIEW EASTWARD from Paradise Divide, at the headwaters of the Slate River, above Crested Butte. The 14,000-foot Maroon Bells peaks, near Aspen, can be seen in the distance.**

**A BEAUTIFUL REFLECTION of distant peaks on one of the alpine tarns can be viewed atop Paradise Divide, north of Crested Butte. This scenic spot offers picturesque camping sites along the road from Pittsburg to Elko.**

Back to the Slate River road and Paradise Divide: The name apparently was derived from the nearby Paradise mine on the west slope of Mount Baldy; however, it is most fitting for the extreme beauty of the location today. Located at the top of the pass — where the road leads over from the Slate River drainage to that of Rock Creek and the Crystal River — are two very beautiful small lakes, which reflect the distant mountains like mirrors on a clear-and-still morning. Numerous campsites are found around the lakes, which offer a true "paradise" of high-country camping possibilities.

The old Yule Pass trail also begins here, but it is only drivable for about a half-mile, until it is completely rock-slid. If you drive on out to the point where it turns into a foot trail, be prepared to back all the way out again. The trail over Yule Pass is very worthwhile. Realization that marble existed in the upper reaches of the Crystal River area took place as far back as 1873, when a geologist by the name of Sylvester Richardson — working for the Hayden Survey — reported his find. A year later, while prospecting for precious metals, George Yule discovered the deposits on the stream that now bears his name.

RICHARD DAIS PHOTO

**THE YULE PASS TRAIL can be seen in the distance in this scene, crossing the talus slopes of Cinnamon Pass, above the deep cañon of the Slate River. The pass itself is located in the low notch in the center of the picture. The pass nearly became the route of a narrow-gauge electric tramway to serve the Yule Marble Company quarry near the town of Marble. It was to have connected with the Denver & Rio Grande Railroad at Anthracite.**

While gold and silver mines were being developed in the Crystal River and Schofield areas, marble deposits gained more and more attention. By 1887, it was fully realized that the commercial value of the marble deposits required a means of transportation.

When the Colorado Marble & Mining Company was formed in 1891, they proceeded to survey for an electric tramway line to the head of Yule Creek, across Yule Pass and on down the Slate River to the Denver & Rio Grande Railroad terminus at Anthracite, above Crested Butte. The tramway never materialized, but the grading work did leave the Yule Pass trail, which we know today. Transportation to Marble eventually was taken care of by the Crystal River & San Juan Railroad, completed in 1906, which connected with the D&RG at Carbondale. Yule Pass today offers a delightful trail from Paradise Pass to the Yule marble quarries above Marble. The views of the surrounding geology are magnificent, and vast fields of wildflowers are found in the high basins of upper Yule Creek. It is suggested that a one-way hike be planned from Paradise Pass if prior arrangements can be made for a waiting

vehicle in the town of Marble. If you hike this old trail across Yule Pass, keep in mind that many years ago the baseball team from Marble used to trek across this pass to meet their competitors in Crested Butte.

One final note on the Yule marble quarry. The old quarry was shut down for the last time in 1941, due to several reasons — none of which was a lack of high-quality marble. The market for marble was waning in favor of granite when a fire destroyed the great marble finishing plant in the town of Marble, and World War II was just beginning at this time. Visits to the abandoned quarry have been fascinating over the years since then, with no one dreaming that it would ever again open for production. Recently, however, the Colorado Yule Marble Company was re-established, and the summer of 1990 found new bridges and roadway being constructed from Marble to the quarry site. On September 15, 1990, the first blocks of marble were trucked out from Marble to the Denver & Rio Grande Western Railroad in Glenwood Springs. Hopefully, a new era has begun for the little town of Marble, Colorado.

173

**THE SINGLE REMAINING CABIN in the ghost town of Elko appears in this view. Elko is in Elko Park, near Schofield Pass. The high, rugged mountain in the background is the back side of the famous Maroon Bells, near the town of Aspen.**

From Paradise Divide, one can drive on down the Rock Creek valley into the townsite of Elko and connect with the Schofield Pass road. Although it is possible to drive a regular automobile up to Paradise from Crested Butte, I suggest a four-wheel-drive vehicle to connect through to Elko. Elko and Schofield parks mark the headwaters of the south fork of the Crystal River. The ghost town of Elko occupies a site near Elko Lake in a beautiful little valley — at an elevation of 10,500 feet — known as Elko Park. It was an early mining camp, which was short-lived during the 1880's and '90's. Today, only a few foundations and one partially standing cabin mark the site. The high 14,000-foot summits of the Maroon Bells are plainly visible to the northeast. From here we will turn left on the Schofield Pass road and follow the Crystal River on down to Crystal City, on what has become one of Colorado's most "notorious" four-wheel-drive roads. Then, we will return to Crested Butte via Schofield Pass and East River.

I strongly urge that those who wish to drive

**THE BACKSIDES** of the famous 14,000-foot Maroon Bells can be seen from the spectacular Hasley Pass trail above Schofield Park.

**BELOW:** Hikers were back-packing through Hasley Basin along the Hasley Pass trail above Schofield. Snowmass Mountain, at 14,093 feet, and Hagerman Peak, at 13,841 feet, dominate this wonderful view of the Elk Mountains across flowery alpine meadows.

**SCHOFIELD PASS, at an elevation of 10,707 feet, connects the headwaters of the East River — flowing southward, toward Crested Butte — with those of Rock Creek, which flows northward, toward Marble. Dominated by sharply pointed Snowmass Mountain, at 14,092 feet, the southern flank of the Elk Mountains can be seen in the background.**

**MOUNT BALDY, at an elevation of 12,805 feet, rises above a beautiful waterfall on the Crystal River, near the townsite of Schofield. The view is seen from the Schofield Pass road as it passes through 10,000-foot Schofield Park.**

**THE ONLY REMAINING structure in the townsite of Schofield looks like this today. This cabin is privately owned by people who offer it for shelter to anyone who might wish to use it. Mount Baldy, at 12,805 feet, rises above 10,000-foot Schofield Park.**

from Schofield Park on down to Crystal be seasoned four-wheelers, as there are potentially dangerous portions of the road ahead. First, the townsite of Schofield is visited in the middle of the park. Like Elko, Schofield never amounted to much, and it was basically finished by the Silver Panic of 1893. Today, a single privately-owned cabin remains, which has been offered to anyone who might need the shelter. A stove and bedsprings are found inside, and if one does not mind sharing the cabin with packrats and mice, a comfortable shelter is available.

For those who like to hike into higher elevations, Schofield Park makes an excellent base from which to begin. One suggestion is the Hasley Pass trail, which follows the East Fork of the Crystal River. The Snowmass Mountain 7$^1$/$_2$-minute USGS

quad map will be helpful as a guide to this high, magnificent viewpoint. Striking views of Snowmass Mountain and the Maroon Bells, as well as the rest of the Elk Mountain Range, may be seen. It is a good place to reflect on the unusual geology of the Elk Mountains. The Maroon Bells, Pyramid Peak and Castle Peak are all part of an uplifted section of Paleozoic sedimentary rock, as opposed to the more commonly found Precambrian igneous that forms Snowmass and Capitol peaks. The striking maroon color and tilted strata of the "Bells" has made them some of the most-often photographed mountains in the entire U.S. The West Maroon Pass trail to Crater and Maroon lakes is also suggested from here.

Following the Crystal River road northwest

**FALLING WATER** provided power for this old concentrating mill at Schofield, near Crested Butte.

**A BEAUTIFUL WATERFALL** is located on the Crystal River, just below the townsite of Schofield. This 1990 photograph was taken from the same angle as the early-day view (above), which shows a hydro-powered ore-concentration mill. This structure was somewhat similar to the so-called "Crystal Mill," still standing today in Crystal City, above Marble.

RON RUHOFF PHOTO

from Schofield now, we soon enter a narrow-and-steep canyon, where caution is advised. Just before the drop-off, there is a beautiful waterfall — on the right — which is the historic site of a large water-powered ore-concentrating mill.

Soon, the road makes a deep ford of the Crystal River, a place where the bridge was washed out many years ago. The water can be very deep, and there is danger of flooding an engine or losing your brakes just when you need them most! Before descending the steep, narrow shelf road past the Devil's Punchbowl waterfalls, test your brakes ahead of time. The Devil's Punchbowl falls are a beautiful sight, but if you stop on the shelf road for photographs, be sure to chock the wheels of your vehicle with rocks, and never depend on parking brakes in such a place. A number of people have lost their lives at this very spot in recent years due to careless driving habits. The best method is to park in the convenient parking area at the bottom of the hill by the bridge, then walk back for photographs of the falls.

RON RUHOFF PHOTOS

**A FORD BRONCO** was fording the Crystal River above the steepest part of the road from Schofield Pass to Crystal City.

**THE "DEVIL'S PUNCHBOWL"** is located on the upper Crystal River, beneath the steepest-and-roughest part ot the road from Schofield Pass to Crystal City. Note: One must be careful of wet brakes on this road before making the steep descent.

THE STEEP four-wheel-drive road above Crystal City leads to Schofield Pass, and it is often covered with the remnant of the Crystal Peak snow-slide — which runs each winter — until it finally melts during late summer. This July day in 1990 finds several jeepers helping one another through the snow with winches, on their way to the pass.

THE SO-CALLED "Crystal Mill" probably is the most-often pictured Colorado ghost-town structure today; however, it was not actually a mill at all. During the gold-and-silver mining days, the Crystal River was dammed to provide water power to run air compressors in this building. This was for the Sheep Mountain Tunnel (mine), located adjacent to this building. Local historical groups and the Ghost Town Club of Colorado have contributed to structural repair of this favorite old building in recent years.

Another problem often exists on the road just below the Devil's Punchbowl. Each year a large snowslide thunders down the slopes of Crystal Mountain and covers the road. It usually does not melt until early August — sometimes even later.

When Crystal City is reached, we are in familiar territory (as covered by the previously footnoted books). It is satisfying to know, however, that the town remains (at this writing), as intact as it has for many years. All privately owned, the original structures, including the schoolhouse, the Crystal Club and the "Crystal River Currant" newspaper office are kept in a fine state of preservation. Even a small store is operated during the summer months for tourists, who usually come up to see the famous "Crystal Mill." The mill itself stands at the western edge of town, in a picturesque pose beside a sparkling waterfall on the Crystal River. The building was actually a water-powered powerhouse for the Sheep Mountain Tunnel. The mill itself is now only a pile of boards off to the right.

**SNOWMASS MOUNTAIN, at an elevation of 14,092 feet, towers over the Crystal River Cañon on the road to Lead King Basin — high above Crystal City.**

**EMERALD LAKE, as seen from the top of 10,707-foot Schofield Pass, gives jeepers this view. Well named for its striking green color, the lake offers excellent fishing on the headwaters of the East River above Gothic.**

Before returning to Schofield Pass, another four-wheel-drive road is worth mentioning. At the eastern edge of Crystal City, one can drive up into Lead King Basin, along the North Fork of the Crystal River. The road winds past early mining country to timberline, where spectacular views of 14,092-foot Snowmass Mountain are visible. This is a favorite backpacking-and-climbing route, with Geneva Lake located a mile above the road. The four-wheel-drive road continues on to Lost Trail Creek — even though not shown on most maps — and it offers a beautiful drive back to Marble along the northern slopes of Sheep Mountain.

Back to Schofield Pass now, which is the right-hand turn in the road, if one is coming down from Paradise Divide. The pass itself crosses to the East River drainage at an elevation of 10,707 feet. Just over the top, a fine view of Emerald Lake is obtained, a favorite camping-and-fishing spot.

**NAMED AFTER GOTHIC MOUNTAIN, the little town of Gothic was a booming mining settlement when this picture was recorded. The mountain called "Crested Butte" is in the far distance. During 1880 the town was thriving, with lots selling for $600 to $1,500 each. This view was photographed during 1887.**

The town of Gothic is reached about half way between Schofield Pass and Crested Butte. It is not truly a ghost town, since it is now entirely owned by the Rocky Mountain Biological Laboratory. The original buildings have been refurbished for use as classrooms and dormatories for those who come here for the study of Colorado's wildlife.

Originally, Gothic was established as a central outfitting camp for the many mines of the district in the 1880's. Close to a thousand people once lived in the mining camp, which took its name from nearby Gothic Mountain. Around the year 1928, Dr. John C. Johnson bought up the entire town for practically nothing and established the Rocky Mountain Biological Laboratory. Dr. Johnson has been gone for many years now, but his dream lives on with fine reputation.

I enjoyed talking with Dr. Johnson on several occasions when I visited Gothic during the 1960's. He loved to tell the story of one of the original in-

GEORGE E. MELLEN PHOTOS – MERLE AND AUDREY DORSETT COLLECTION

**THE TWO HISTORIC VIEWS on this page show early-day scenes in the mining camp of Gothic. This camp is now the location of the Rocky Mountain Biological Laboratory.**

habitants of Gothic, a miner by the name of Garwood Judd. Mr. Judd came here in the 1880's, when the town was just being formed, and he stayed until his death in 1930. Per his wishes, Garwood Judd's ashes were scattered over the surrounding countryside. Perhaps as a good-luck charm, Dr. Johnson always carried a piece of bone in his pocket, alledgedly from Judd's remains, and he enjoyed showing it to those who would listen to his stories.

The old Copper Creek road, which leads directly out of Gothic to the east, is now closed to vehicular travel, but it is well worth the short hike to beautiful Judd Falls. The Copper Creek trail continues on to the Sylvanite mine, one of the area's largest.

**DR. JOHN C. JOHNSON (left) and an unidentified instructor posed on the front porch of one of Gothic's original buildings during August of 1964. Dr. Johnson organized the Rocky Mountain Biological Laboratory in Gothic during 1928, utilizing the existing structures of the old mining camp for labs and dorms. Today, the RMB Laboratory remains in Gothic, fulfilling the dreams of Dr. Johnson. Located in a colorful mountain setting enjoyed by many students every summer, young people pursue a knowledge of Colorado's high-country wildlife.**

RON RUHOFF PHOTO

185

RON RUHOFF PHOTOS

**"LEE'S TAVERN"** — as this old saloon was known, by the sign over its door in 1949 — remains today as Gothic's most often photographed building. It has often been incorrectly called a "hotel" or "town hall."

**THE HOME** of the late Dr. John C. Johnson, director of the Rocky Mountain Biological Laboratory in Gothic, as it appeared in 1959.

Those who enjoy backpacking can continue on up to Copper Lake and over East Maroon Pass to East Maroon Lake, eventually coming out on the highway from Aspen to Maroon Lake. West Maroon Pass offers a spectacular trail from Schofield Park to Crater and Maroon lakes, where wonderful views of the 14,000-foot Maroon Bells are obtained.

The return to Crested Butte from Gothic may be made via either the main road through the Mount Crested Butte ski village, or by following the East River on down to the Brush Creek road. Skiing has been popular on Crested Butte for many years, but with the development of modern ski lifts and facilities, the Crested Butte area has become one of Colorado's most popular ski resorts. In 1974, the village of Mount Crested Butte was incorporated, and it now serves the needs of skiers who wish to live and shop right next to the slopes. [*Ed. Note:* The name "Mount Crested Butte" is an anomaly because the word "butte" means "a flat-topped hill with steep slopes, which stands by itself, i.e., a small mesa." Hence, the word "mount" in the name is superfluous.]

RON RUHOFF PHOTOS

**JUDD FALLS,** a half-mile above Gothic, is located on Copper Creek. The waterfall was named for Garwood Judd, last old-time resident of Gothic — who passed away in 1930. Per his wishes, his ashes were scattered across the nearby mountains, which he loved so fondly.

**THIS SKI RESORT,** strangely called "Mount Crested Butte," was incorporated in 1974. It is shown here, nestled on the north slope of the resort's lofty 12,162-foot namesake, scenic Crested Butte.

**JEEPING OVER PEARL PASS, between Crested Butte and Ashcroft, the jagged ridges of 14,265-foot Castle Peak — Colorado's twelfth-highest mountain and most lofty of all the Elk Range summits — are seen in the view above. Pearl Pass is often snowed-in until late summer, and it offers difficult four-wheeling in many sections, but it is all worth the effort for the fabulous views from its summit.**

Two fascinating four-wheel-drive roads lead east from Crested Butte, one over Pearl Pass to Ashcroft and Aspen, and the other one reaching Taylor Park via Cement Creek and Italian Mountain. The Brush Creek road leaves Highway 135 two miles south of Crested Butte, and it first traverses about five miles of private ranchland before entering the national forest. You may find it necessary to open (and close behind you) some livestock gates along the way. Once above timberline, the views become spectacular in all directions. Uncompahgre Peak can be seen in the San Juans, far to the south. And once atop 12,705-foot Pearl Pass, the views of nearby 14,265-foot Castle Peak and Cathedral Peak are worth the entire journey. Part way down Pearl Pass, one can drive the old wagon road

to the Montezuma mine, high in Montezuma Basin, directly beneath Castle Peak.

Snowfields will probably still cover portions of the Pearl Pass road until late summer, and it is advisable to ask locally about the condition of the road before counting on driving all the way over to Aspen.

Once down to Ashcroft, on Castle Creek, the road is paved and open year-around on into Aspen. Today, the many buildings in Ashcroft are maintained by the Aspen Historical Society, and during the summer, attendants are there to answer questions. The Aspen Cross-Country Ski School utilizes the area each winter, and many marked trails and warming huts are available for those who wish to buy a ski ticket.

THE VIEW ABOVE is of Ashcroft, as it looked during the summer of 1976. In 1883, Ashcroft had a population of 1,000, and it was a far busier mining camp than nearby Aspen for awhile. When Aspen became a Denver & Rio Grande Railroad terminal in 1887, Ashcroft began a downhill slide. The last inhabitant, a hermit named Jack Leahy, hung on until his death in 1939.

ASHCROFT'S "HOTEL VIEW" looked like this after restoration in 1974 by the Aspen Historical Society. The old structure had collapsed during the winter of 1970, which prompted the restoration of the entire ghost town. Today, Ashcroft is accessible year-round on a paved highway from Aspen.

**A COLORFUL DAY in 1959 was photographed atop 11,928-foot Taylor Pass. Cathedral Pcak rises to a height of 13,943 feet in the background — above Montezuma Basin. Taylor Pass remains a delightful crossing today between Taylor Park and Aspen, via the ghost town of Ashcroft. Historically, this pass was the main route to the early mines of Ashcroft before Aspen became accessible via the narrow-gauge Denver & Rio Grande Railroad.**

Rather than back-track to Crested Butte to describe the Cement Creek road to Italian Mountain, we will make a circle journey by including Taylor Pass. This four-wheel-drive road begins at the northern edge of the Ashcroft townsite and offers easy driving to the 11,928-foot pass. Taylor Pass offers spectacular views to the west of the Cathedral and Castle Peak area, and to the south, are alpine Taylor Lake and distant Taylor Park.

The road continues down from the headwaters of the Taylor River to the main Taylor Park road. This side of the pass will probably prove to be rougher than the Ashcroft side. Continue about two and a half miles, past the Dorchester campground, and turn right on the Italian Creek road. Italian Creek and the entire Taylor Park area is prime fishing and hunting country, and numerous campsites can be found without the need for using official campgrounds. Automobiles can drive up Italian Creek for about a mile before a sign warns "Four-Wheel-Drive Only."

The four-wheel-drive road leads up to a pass that has never been officially named, but most agree it should be called Italian Pass. It crosses between the Taylor River and Cement Creek drainages, halfway between two spectacular mountains — North Italian Mountain, 13,225 feet, and American Flag Mountain, 12,720 feet. The road originally served the Italian Mountain mining district — in particular, the Star mine on the northern side of the peak. American Flag Mountain shows a ragged eastern face, with strata and coloring that make it appear somewhat like an American Flag. It is visible from Taylor Park and the beginning of the Italian Creek road.

Italian Pass crosses at an elevation of 11,997 feet, and it offers a place to drive your vehicle out on a point, somewhat reminiscent of "Oh! Point" on the San Juan's Engineer Pass, where a wide panoramic view shows the entire Sawatch Range and Taylor Park to the east.

The road next leads to the head of Spring Creek

RON RUHOFF PHOTOS

**THE VIEWPOINT from atop 11,997-foot Italian Pass looked like this during the summer of 1990. Here, you are looking toward the southwest, across Taylor Park, toward the Sawatch Range. Although never officially named, "Italian Pass" offers an easy four-wheel-drive crossing from Taylor Park to Crested Butte.**

**IN THE SCENE BELOW, you are on Reno Divide, looking toward the northeast. Crystal Mountain (12,777 feet), Hunters Hill (12,618 feet), Taylor Peak (13,435 feet) and Mount Tilton (12,462 feet) can be seen in the distance. Reno Divide crosses between the Cement Creek and Spring Creek drainages.**

canyon, headwaters of present-day Spring Creek Reservoir, past the old Stewart mine to a notable fork in the road. The right-hand fork follows the original road along a rough, rocky shelf, where hand-laid rock still holds the grade. When I first drove Italian Pass over 20 years ago, this was the only route, but it has been replaced in recent years by a newer road that descends Spring Creek some distance to circle the rocky slopes of Italian Mountain. The newer road is the left fork, and it is the suggested way to travel. In the summer of 1990, I drove both routes to see if the old one was still passable. And while it is still drivable, I found it extremely rough and potentially damaging to a vehicle.

The road crosses "Reno Divide" next, taking you from the Spring Creek drainage to that of Cement Creek. A livestock gate must be opened before driving down to the main Cement Creek road. The old original rocky route meets the newer road right next to the gate.

Once down to Cement Creek, you may want to follow that road upstream to the North Italian Mountain area. Again, there is more beautiful scenery to behold.

RON RUHOFF PHOTOS

**AMERICAN FLAG MOUNTAIN,** with a fresh coat of autumn snow, which emphasizes the striations on its east face, gives the appearance of the stripes of the American flag. The 12,713-foot peak was viewed by the photographer from the junction of Italian Creek and the Taylor River.

**FOUR-WHEELING** on the original Italian Pass road across the rocky southern slope of Italian Mountain is extremely rough and dangerous. A new road has been constructed in recent years to bypass this old "frame-twister."

Cement Creek offers numerous camping possibilities and good fishing all the way down to Colorado Highway 135, where it comes out six miles south of Crested Butte.

This completes a description of the most significant adventure trails of northern Gunnison County. As you can see, with Crested Butte as a base, there are a great number of possible circle trips over high passes, as well as roads and trails that one can drive and hike. The area is unsurpassed anywhere in Colorado for history and rugged, colorful scenery.

**Acknowledgements:**

Audrey and Merle Dorsett, having lived in Crested Butte from 1949 until 1980, operated the Skyland Camp for 29 years. They have been most helpful with their photographs and knowledge of the area.

Thanks also to Robert L. Brown, Richard Dais and Jack L. Morison for photographs supplied.

Additional information from *The Gunnison Country,* by Duane Vandenbusch, *Stampede to Timberline,* by Muriel Wolle, *The Colorado Pass Book,* by Don Koch, *When Coal Was King,* by Duane A. Smith, and the many previously published books from **Sundance Publications, Ltd.,** of Denver, Colorado.